THE
FINANCIAL
DIET

THE
FINANCIAL
DIET

A Total Beginner's Guide
to Getting Good with Money

Chelsea Fagan
Designed by Lauren Ver Hage

Illustrations by Eve Mobley

A Holt Paperback
Henry Holt and Company
New York

Holt Paperbacks

Henry Holt and Company

Publishers since 1866
175 Fifth Avenue
New York, New York 10010
www.henryholt.com

A Holt Paperback® and ® are registered trademarks of
Macmillan Publishing Group, LLC.

Library of Congress Cataloging-in-Publication Data

Names: Fagan, Chelsea, author. | Ver Hage, Lauren, author.
Title: The financial diet : a total beginner's guide to getting good with
   money / Chelsea Fagan ; designed by Lauren Ver Hage.
Description: First edition. | New York : Henry Holt and Company, [2018]
Identifiers: LCCN 2017027973 | ISBN 9781250176165 (pbk.)
Subjects: LCSH: Finance, Personal. | Women—Finance, Personal.
Classification: LCC HG179 .F324 2018 | DDC 332.024—dc23
LC record available at https://lccn.loc.gov/2017027973

Our books may be purchased in bulk for promotional, educational, or
business use. Please contact your local bookseller or the Macmillan Corporate
and Premium Sales Department at (800) 221-7945, extension 5442, or by e-mail
at MacmillanSpecialMarkets@macmillan.com.

First Edition 2018

Designed by Lauren Ver Hage
Illustrations by Eve Mobley

Printed in the United States of America

11 10 9 8

To Marc and Joe,
who were there when it was hardest,
and there when it was most lovely.

Author's note.

This book is intended solely as a source of inspiration and information for readers who wish to take charge of creating a healthier financial future for themselves. Examples of typical financial situations and solutions to common problems are included for illustrative purposes only. If the reader needs advice concerning the evaluation and management of specific legal or financial risks or liabilities, such as bankruptcy or tax matters, he or she should seek the help of a licensed, knowledgeable professional.

Contents

*Note: glossary terms are highlighted in yellow.

THE
FINANCIAL
DIET

Introduction:

How to Give a Shit About Money

Saving money
isn't about depriving
yourself. It's about
deciding you love
Future You as
much as you love
Today You.

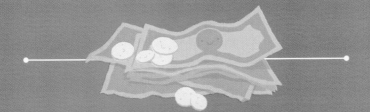

I graduated from high school when I was seventeen years old. The subprime mortgage crisis hadn't yet happened, and it was a very good time to be a teenager who was irresponsible with money. When bankers weren't standing on the roof of their branches and throwing loans at anyone who walked by, they were going into the high schools to find unsuspecting teens to ask them if they wanted a credit card. And looking back, when you compare the potential implications of a starter credit card to the student loans those same kids were signing on to, getting a Visa with a $500 limit was probably the least of their worries, but still, handing out a credit card to someone whose primary "life skills" education came from episodes of *Degrassi* still seems pretty cruel. Of course we all wanted free money, and of course we were going to pay it back on time. We were teenagers, and we had zero concept of fiscal responsibility and every interest in instant gratification. I was definitely one of those teenagers.

The day I turned eighteen, I acquired my little card full of free money, and maxed it out within a month and a half of delirious spending. Once swiping it no longer provided me with the sweet, sweet Forever 21 dresses my body craved, I tossed that bad boy into the garbage and ignored the increasingly urgent notices that arrived in the mail. After all, I had a savings account with thousands of dollars from my summer jobs to blow through. You couldn't touch Teenage Chelsea!

By the time the financial crisis hit in 2008, and banks were no longer the tire fire of free money they once were, I'd already defaulted on my card (which meant tanking my credit score and being hounded by collection agencies), blown through my savings, and was left with absolutely zero resources when it came time to get my shit together and start community college. But because my parents put a significant amount of caveats on any potential loan cosigning (excellent grades job-ready majors, prestigious yet inexpensive schools), I ended up going to France for school instead of somewhere in the United States when it came time to transfer from community college—in France, I didn't need them.

Looking back, I am grateful they prevented me from signing on the dotted line for the $50,000-per-year dream school I desperately wanted to attend. I came out of my education with just a few grand in subsidized government loans, which I went on to pay off in minuscule amounts each month. Sure, I have no degree—I was lucky to be hired at my first full-time job before I finished school in France—but given how I started, I consider myself lucky to be where I am today.

It was nuts that as a dumb teenager I was allowed to make enormous financial decisions that would impact the rest of my adult life. I wasn't equipped to pick a color scheme for my wardrobe, let alone determine what my budget would look like twenty years down the road. I mostly have my parents' reluctance to cosign a college loan to thank for my relatively healthy finances today, and the luck of landing a job that cut off my education spending early. However, I did have the good sense to pay off that defaulted Visa when I was twenty-two by taking huge chunks out of my first several paychecks and settling with the collection agency for a lower amount. I realize that my problems weren't exactly universal, but I also know that navigating the fallout of financial mistakes we make when we are young is pretty much guaranteed. The story of a financially troubled youth is a familiar one, and many people in my generation who did make the decision to go to college are now saddled with five or six figures of student debt before they even get a job.

It's true that the system has just been stacked against us. I mean, if an idiot like me can be doing all right, and my friend from high school who spent half her time getting straight As and the other half volunteering can be in severe debt, nothing means anything anymore. Which is why it can be so easy to just throw our hands up in the air and say "fuck it" to the idea of ever being good with money. And it doesn't help that the information available about personal finance oscillates between a less fun version of your dad yelling at you about stocks, and tone-deaf articles about #millennials not buying homes (it's because we have billions of dollars of student debt, asshole). It often feels easier to just excuse yourself from the conversation.

For me, the rejection of all things #finance and #wealth meant that I also rejected the idea of being a competent adult with some control over her life. Yes, I rented an apartment of my own, had a salary, and even those elusive "benefits" I heard my parents mention, but that didn't mean I was capable of creating a budget or deciding what to do with the money I actually had. Words like "investment" and "IRA" scared the hell out of me, and the only thing I was really capable of doing, money-wise, was hoarding it all in a checking account. Even on the rare occasions that I had what I (humbly) considered to be a lot of money at once, I had no idea how to "make my money work for me." In my early twenties, the only actual investment I made was in an Italian designer purse bought in a fugue state in a department store. I managed to make it halfway through the decade without anything concrete to show for it, besides a couple grand in checking and a one-bedroom apartment filled with IKEA furniture.

On paper, though, I had achieved a lot by age twenty-five: I had a job I was proud of, I had a strong relationship and friendships, and the financial indiscretions of my youth were largely behind me. But it dawned on me that I was judging my current self on what were the comically low standards I had set for my former self, and I was allowing myself to believe that "not a train wreck" was the same as "actively good with money." So I started a little Tumblr to track my budget and hold myself accountable. I called it The Financial Diet, because I didn't want to keep treating my financial health the way I was treating my body—by eating an entire bag of Kettle Cooked Jalapeño Chips at night and then wondering why I felt like I'd been punched in the face the next morning. I knew that the key to becoming better with money would only be found through balance and thoughtful decision-making. I also knew that just like I wasn't going to become one of those women who does CrossFit competitions while eight months pregnant, I wasn't going to become some high-powered money manager, either. And beyond establishing a firm foundation with money, in developing The Financial Diet, I've learned countless surprising things about myself (that I hope will be helpful to you), like "it's worth it to pay professionals to do shit you don't know how to do and will put off until it's too late," and "do not fear Excel spreadsheets, for they are your friends." I can say with confidence that today I am much better and smarter when it comes to money—and the general act of living well—than I ever was before.

And perhaps the most important lesson I've drawn from creating TFD, both personally and financially, has been how crucial it is that you surround yourself with good people. We talk constantly on the site about how important a good money community is, friends and loved ones and experts to hold you accountable and to help one another to grow. When I founded TFD, my partner Lauren Ver Hage (she designed this whole book you're currently reading!) joined me on day three, and now we are a small team of five women who publish hundreds more women (and occasionally guys!) from around the world every year. We solicit the advice and the feedback of experts constantly and have rounded up more than twenty of our favorite money experts (and just general favorite humans!) to make this book. Not all of our (or our experts') opinions completely match up, and you

The Agony And The Ecstasy Of Cleaning Out Your Closet

I have spent a significant amount of time getting rid of clothes these last few weeks, and a small amount of time acquiring them. In my mind, when I imagine my wardrobe and the space it should occupy in my life, I now think largely in terms of proportions. I want a certain amount of this, a certain amount of that, and no waste. When I looked over the amo...

The very first Tumblr draft of TFD...yikes

will see that this book is full of tons of different advice for different needs and goals, but the point is that we are all openly having this conversation. We are asking the questions, and being open with one another, and sharing the hard lessons we have learned. Just like I never would have been able to build TFD without Lauren and our team, you will never get good with money if you have to go it totally alone. Surrounding yourself with people who make you better is key

Being smart with money isn't just about what you put in the bank, it's about everything from the clothes you put in your closet to the food you put in your kitchen (and actually cook, instead of ordering Seamless . . . again). Learning basic skills like how to install a shelf or pick out a jacket that will last more than one New York winter has done more for me financially than any raise on a biweekly paycheck. The way we live today dictates everything about the kind of life we will have tomorrow, and even though this cliché was a painful one for me to accept, a dollar not wasted is just as good as a dollar earned.

I thought that because I'd ruined my credit when I was eighteen, I was doomed to spend my twenties treading water. But I am proud to say that I now have a credit score that is edging into the "good" territory, and I didn't have to do anything painful to make it happen. I am also someone who is now capable of setting a budget for herself and saving money as well. I've learned where I can do things myself and when I need to ask for help (such as with taxes). Even as a #millennial whose financial starting point was far from perfect, I've learned how to get my shit together, and it is incredibly satisfying.

If you are the kind of person who wants to become better with money—and I assume you are, because you bought (or stole) this book—I promise, the solution is probably simpler than you think. It starts with figuring out where you are, being honest about what you could be doing better, and starting with the smallest possible steps toward better-ness. It's good to think big, of course (and it's good to have goals for years and even decades down the road, eventually), but the only way to get control over your life is to start small. Your first step can be something as simple as reading this book, so congratulations! You're on your way.

The way I started small was just with talking about money. This meant asking questions and not being afraid of looking stupid (which I was, of course, about money). I started bringing up the topic of savings and salaries and 401(k)s at brunch with my friends, and I was surprised by how much everyone was interested in talking about it. Once that seal was broken, and it was established that talking about money was *not* taboo, everyone had a story to tell. Everyone wanted to ask a question they'd been struggling with or get the table's opinion on a crucial financial decision (and maybe that two-Bloody-Mary buzz didn't hurt, either).

When I started those conversations, it quickly became clear that many of us (my former self included) don't even really know what things like investments are. I mean, yeah, okay, I saw *The Wolf of Wall Street*, but could I have given you a working definition of a stock or a bond? Did I know what IRA stands for (individual retirement account)? Did I have any other plans for retirement besides "die before my bad money choices can catch up to me?" Of course not. I didn't think I'd ever be the kind of person to own property or invest in things. And while this initially made me feel like an enormous loser, in talking about money with my friends I quickly learned that it actually made me pretty average. How many people in my generation were living debt-free, or buying property, or establishing something referred to as an "estate"? Anecdotally, not a ton of them. And the statistics mostly backed that up.

Millennials & Money

First-time homeowners currently make up

32 PERCENT OF ALL BUYERS

the lowest since 1987—compared with a historical average of 40 percent.
—*NERD WALLET*

Twentysomethings carry an average of

45k

in debt. —*BUSINESS INSIDER*

FEWER THAN

50%

OF MILLENNIALS ARE SAVING FOR RETIREMENT

—*MONEY UNDER 30*

Today about a third of eighteen-to-thirty-four-year-olds

live with their parents. And for the first time since at least 1880, a greater share of this age group is bunking up with Mom and Dad than living in any other arrangement (such as dwelling alone, with a roommate, or with a spouse or romantic partner). —*WASHINGTON POST*

In talking about money with people (once I started paying attention to money, I wanted to talk about it all the time), I learned that pretty much every single person I knew had at least one obvious thing they could be doing differently. Some of them were very "fucking, duh," such as "stop buying ten-dollar bottled designer juices twice a day because they make you feel like a better person," but others weren't so obvious. It wasn't until a friend told me she made it a rule to transfer her savings automatically when her paycheck hit so she would never "see" the money that I realized it was seeing that original number in my account that made me feel so bad about moving it over into savings. Once a friend confessed to me that she was so heavily in debt that if she didn't find several thousand dollars in the next month or so, she'd have to move out of New York and back in with her parents. And bear in mind, this is a friend with whom I regularly went out for coffees, drinks, dinners, and other city-dwelling social activities that center around overpriced food and alcohol. I was shocked, of course, but mostly I felt disappointed that she felt she couldn't tell anyone until it had gotten that bad. And while some crusty old "finance expert" might have a list of a million things she could have done better to avoid this—starting with forgoing her daily Starbucks addiction—it felt unhelpful to criticize what was already done. I realized that she probably hadn't told anyone because she was afraid of being judged. But instead of judging, her situation made me think about the social pressure to spend money that is so deeply entrenched in the way many of us live our lives, especially in a city. It's extremely difficult *not* to indulge in all of the things that lead a person to have $30 in her savings account. But I promise you, the chances that there isn't at least one thing in *your* life that could be immediately (easily!) improved, when it comes to your finances, are probably zero.

We live in a world that encourages us to spend wastefully, accumulate more than we need, and put off things like retirement savings until . . . we're basically retired. It's easy to look around us and see all the things we could be buying to become the person we want to be, and treat fiscal responsibility like the exclusive domain of antisocial dweebs. But in developing and running TFD every day, I have realized that the first concrete steps to becoming the kind of person who is "good with money" are rather easy and straightforward—these are the basics of getting good with money in a year that we have learned in three years of building The Financial Diet, and being on serious financial diets ourselves:

How to Get Good with Money in a Year

#1. CREATE A BUDGET

Without a budget, you have no chance of getting control over your money—and getting it to do what you want. Sit down with a few months' worth of card statements and bills, track exactly what you're doing, and sort everything into a category going forward.

#2. BUILD AN EMERGENCY FUND

We recommend that you have three months' worth of all living costs saved up in an easily accessible, regular savings account. You can do up to six months' worth, but, at least initially, three months is the best balance between "doable" and "providing the necessary security." This emergency fund (and about $1,000 in your checking account for day-to-day use, once bills are paid) are really the only money you should keep in regular bank accounts. The rest of your savings should go to much more useful and valuable things, like retirement (but more on that later).

#3. DO A CREDIT CARD CHECKUP

Comb through statements and purchases from the last three months, and make sure you're not utilizing more than 30% of your available credit (this impacts your credit score), and raise your limits if you can (and if you trust yourself) to grow the gap between "what you can use" and "what you do use"—, you want as much unused credit as possible. Determine if the rewards systems (travel, cash back, etc.) you have are the most valuable to you, and if you're using them to their fullest extent. Last, set up your bills to be paid on your credit card each month, then set up an automated payment from your checking account to your credit cards to pay them in full each month—this ensures you maximize the rewards you get with money you were already spending.

#4. AUTOMATE WHAT YOU CAN

Card payments, bill payments, and savings transfers should all be automatically made from your checking account. This way, you won't tempt yourself to not save, nor will you take a credit score hit by forgetting to pay something.

#5. KNOW (AND BUILD) YOUR CREDIT SCORE

Use a free online service such as CreditKarma to find out what your credit score is—and many such services will also tell you how to improve it. Check your score at least twice a year—always with soft inquiries, unlike hard credit checks, which happen when you try to get approved for something—and set challenges to yourself to see how high you can get it (and keep it).

#6. PLAN FOR RETIREMENT

Lay out a basic plan for retirement savings. This may sound daunting, but if your employer offers retirement accounts, you can simply set a meeting with your human resources rep to go over your options. Initially, open at least one retirement account based on your needs (there are seven types of retirement accounts, for different needs). After your emergency fund (three to six months' worth of living expenses) is set up, your retirement fund is the first place you're allocating savings.

#7. RUN A CAREER CHECKUP

Compare your salary against others in your field using sites such as Glassdoor. Ask yourself serious questions about your job fulfillment and performance (Are you happy? Are you working toward something specific? Do you see areas to grow in your current job and at your current place of employment?). Brainstorm ways you could improve and brush up on what you could be doing better—from individual tasks to general career development. Set goals for one, five, and ten years down the road in your professional life, and write them down.

#8. ADD AT LEAST ONE SOURCE OF EXTRA INCOME

There are endless side jobs and gigs out there to supplement income, bolster savings, hone new skills, or even make a career transition. Even if you just dedicate a few hours a month to a side job, even one additional stream of income has a huge impact. Whether you're babysitting or tutoring English from bed via Skype or working a full-on part-time job, always have at least one side hustle on the burner.

#9. TREAT YOURSELF

Set mini-goals for yourself across a number of areas (think things like savings, career growth, or personal development) and reward yourself when you hit them. Whether it's a well-earned massage, cocktail, vacation, or fancy dinner, take time for sensible self-care and treat yourself for the milestones you've hit—it will make doing the right thing for yourself most of the time feel manageable, intuitive, and even enjoyable.

These are the basic steps we've developed over the life of TFD. I will go over each in more detail in the following chapters, but I promise you that taking the time to think through these steps will set you up with the right skills (and develop that delayed-gratification muscle) to make life for Future You a whole lot easier.

Coming from someone who went from being the kind of person who ignored collection notices to the kind of person who regularly meets with an accountant, I know from personal experience that the more control I got over my financial life, the more I realized that I am not my mistakes—and neither are you. Giving a shit about money doesn't seem fun, but ultimately it's the most liberating thing you can do with your otherwise chaotic young adult life. It feels like regaining control of a sled that was careening down a snowy mountain.

We at The Financial Diet want to empower you to make your own choices, to build a life intentionally and thoughtfully, and to be able to handle shit if you ever find yourself in an unfortunate financial position. We don't want you to be totally devastated by two months of unemployment, or feel stuck in an unhealthy relationship because it's your only way to afford rent. We want you to be able to decide if and when you want a family, or to travel, or to start a business, and financially, to be able to make it happen.

To help set you on a financial diet to create the life you want, I've brought along experts in every category—from career gurus to chefs to bankers to stylists. We'll break down all those investment terms and strategies that make you want to curl up in a ball. We'll even address what you need to know about mortgages to make home buying not the most terrifying thing on your life to-do list.

None of us should give up the excitement and spontaneity of young adulthood, but we should be going about it in a thoughtful way, so that the fun doesn't come to a screeching halt the second we want to settle down with some security. Because one day you are going to either wish you had been smarter about how you worked, lived, and saved—or be incredibly glad that you were so savvy while you were young.

BUDGET

Chapter 1

How to Make the Most of What You Have

Money without a budget is like champagne without a glass.

I've always been allergic to the word "budget." I spent so long in relative financial chaos, just getting to the point where I wasn't spending in a cycle of anxiety and impulse felt like a victory. To put something as stuffy and restricting as a "budget" on my month-to-month financial life felt like a punishment. I just felt good about the small progress I'd made, so I decided that it was good enough to just always have "something" in my checking account.

That "something" varied wildly, of course, and it never amounted to an actual emergency fund, nor did it ever migrate into an actual savings account—because I didn't have one. I just thought that having over $1,000 in my checking account at all times meant I didn't really *need* a budget. Besides, taking on freelance projects occasionally resulted in large-ish influxes of money outside my regular salary, so I thought that the "real" savings would happen in large, unexpected chunks. I thought that it was good enough to be "good enough" and that not having a defaulted credit card or creditors harassing me was license to never think about something as boring and tedious as a budget.

I didn't want to give in to the idea that there were certain rules I needed to live by—or worse, that I had to impose them on myself. The worst thing about being an adult is the fact that we can do basically whatever we want. You can have Chicken McNuggets and champagne for dinner, but you know that the next day you'll feel like a whoopee cushion made of alcohol and sodium. Yeah, adulthood. The self-imposed restriction on my lifestyle that a budget implied was what made me feel like a failure (also, it was boring). And while letting go of that last little bit of my Peter Pan lifestyle was not easy, it was totally necessary.

Hence, a budget. And because the idea of having to manually enter numbers into a spreadsheet felt very much like the remedial math class I took (and failed!) during summer school in the eleventh grade, my budget started with an app. I downloaded a program called Mint, which basically took all my spending habits and disparate accounts and gathered them into one convenient place, where I could learn about my tendency to blow thousands of dollars a month on eating out, or spend $170 in a shopping frenzy at an outlet store with no recollection of what I had bought. It was a slap in the face to see my impulse spending and bad habits clearly, but great insight as well, as my first budget told me that I would be able to comfortably retire— provided I died within a week.

Whether you have a stable monthly paycheck or work in an industry where your pay is more irregular, there is a series of "Don't You Fucking Dare"s that will help ease you into budgeting and keep you on track before you have to get into the nitty-gritty of a detailed personal budget. When I moved from my regular nine-to-five to running TFD full-time, it meant dry months and unpredictable income. I couldn't have a normal "budget" per se, so I found these rules indispensable in ensuring that those first wobbly years of starting my own business wouldn't result in reverting to my worst habits.

Chelsea's
Don't You
Fucking Dares

1.

DYFD exceed your ability to pay shit back within a month.

The biggest and most foundational rule of a budget—no matter how big the numbers are or how steady your income is—is staying within your own ability to pay things back at the end of the month. Credit cards are something that should be used to your advantage (to build credit; to get miles, points, or cash back; to have more flexibility about when you can buy certain things), but this only works when they are treated as a slightly upgraded version of a debit card. The day you start spending money you can't pay in full at the end of the month (even if you think you're "good for it") is the day you start sabotaging yourself.

2.

DYFD let yourself slip into a "CEO lifestyle."

This might sound dumb, but when I finally embraced the fact that I was actually a chief executive officer of something, it was hard not to slip into this feeling of "I deserve this expensive thing that I shouldn't be buying because I work so hard and look at all I'm accomplishing!" I once very nearly bought myself a $150 facial because I felt that CEOs didn't have acne scars. Well, guess what? I'm a CEO and I have acne scars! The things we think we "need" to fulfill our lifestyles—manicures, daily iced coffees, new shoes, expensive cocktails—are not always actually necessary. Whatever your version of CEO is—whatever person you think you can spend your way into being—you need to get over it. It can be helpful to remind yourself on a regular basis that you shouldn't spend on luxuries just because you *think* that's the life you should be living. This realization was a big step for me.

3.

DYFD not check your account balance at least twice a week.

One of the worst habits I had, which often got me into cycles of impulse spending, was that I *never* checked my account balance. I would basically close my eyes and pray every time my card was swiped, and assumed that as long as my card wasn't getting declined, things were going pretty well. Not having to confront the details of my spending habits, and not knowing the patterns that were underpinning my financial mistakes, allowed me to feel less guilty about it all, much like when you eat the entire cake and don't look at the nutrition facts because you don't have to technically know you're consuming an entire day's worth of calories in one dessert. You can't be on a financial diet unless you force yourself to confront the nutrition facts of your spending habits, no matter how gruesome they might be that first time you take a look around your transaction history.

4.

DYFD think savings are going to happen magically.

I used to believe I would start saving money at some indeterminate date in the future—like when I got an influx of money from a job, or when I reached a magic age when I would become "responsible." I imagined my current self and future self as two very distinct people, and therefore I was always happy to shunt the responsibility of savings off onto the future Chelsea, who would be getting fistfuls of cash and suddenly be motivated to put it into things like emergency funds. But that was absurd—there was one Chelsea, and she needed to start saving.

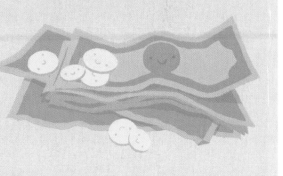

When you start out as a bit of a hot mess (which we all are, at some point), you need to take baby steps to become really good with money. No shame in that. And besides, the truth of making a really good budget—even if you are starting from a point of general fiscal responsibility—is that you have to be hard on yourself. This means

Bank Account Pyramid

TOP

Checking Account Where You Keep Your $1,000 for Day-to-Day

MIDDLE

Basic Savings Account Where You Keep Your Emergency Fund, Immediately Accessible

SECOND-TO-LAST

Semiliquid Savings Accounts—CDs, Time Deposits, and so on (good for things like saving up to buy a house in the next few years, and other medium-term savings)

BOTTOM

Longer-Term Investments

being honest about where your weaknesses are, where you could be saving more money but aren't, how you could be earning more, and what you have a tendency to lie to yourself about. Even if it's just the fact that you buy a cup of coffee on your way to work every day (the personal finance blogging world's Ultimate Sin), there's a vice you could cut back on in a relatively painless way. You just have to take a pair of glasses and tweezers (metaphorically, of course) to your account statements and resolve to be ruthlessly honest. It was only through that exercise that I was able to create my mini-list of DYFDs and from there to build an actual budget.

But once you have your DYFDs mastered, and understand the underlying principles behind budgeting, it's time to draft up a basic budget for making the most with what you have. Not everyone is going to have the same goals or options, but everyone can use a program to track their spending, set reasonable goals, and hold themselves accountable. I personally prefer to use an app to manage my budget because Excel spreadsheets make me break out in hives (I use Mint, but You Need A Budget is another great one). But doing your budget manually is a great activity all of us should force ourselves to undertake at least once. Typing in those numbers by hand does wonders for making you realize what you're spending on (much like doing an all-cash diet for a month). Lucky for us, Lauren is a hard-core Excel budgeter and has shared her universal template for budgeting here.

Lauren's
Budgeting Tracker

STEP 1: Track all sources of *income*. These numbers should reflect your income after tax. Add a "Total" cell at the bottom so you can see what you've brought in that month in full.

STEP 2: Next, calculate all your month's *expenditures*—everything from rent, to groceries, to utilities, dog food, cell phone bill, shopping. It's great to use your credit card and debit card statements as a reference, and go through old receipts. Add a "Total" at the bottom.

STEP 3: Next, track all of your *automated savings*. Note what you portion out for emergency fund, retirement savings. These percentages will vary for everyone, depending on what their goals are and how aggressively they save for retirement (and if you're not saving in any of these categories, you should be—more on that later). Add a "Total" cell at the bottom so you can see what you pay out.

STEP 4: The final step is to simply calculate the *leftover money* that remains in your budget—that illustrates your financial flexibility for the month.

Visit
TheFinancialDiet.com/BookResources to Download

This simple formula isn't perfect—no one budget strategy will work for everyone—but it gives you a good place to start, and, more important, it forces you to confront your habits and weak spots by entering them manually. We recommend that you make this budget manually for at least three months' worth of expenses. Once you have them all laid out, go through and see where you are spending and what your key percentages are: How much are you spending on rent? Food? Shopping? Could you be paying down more debt to save on interest? Most important, how much are you saving each month?

A popular system for breaking down any healthy budget is the 50/30/20 system: with 50 percent of your income going to fixed costs like rent, phone, and utilities; 30 percent of your incoming going to variable/lifestyle-based costs, like groceries, going out, and travel; and 20 percent going to savings, both long- and short-term. The other categories may vary a bit, but 20 percent of your income toward savings is a goal almost everyone should have.

If you look at your last few months' worth of budget and see that your rent is eating up half your income or that you are barely saving, it's time to reassess your lifestyle and do some serious cutting. We recommend updating your budget in this way at least once a year.

The truth is, many of us have a hard time giving savings the full, vigorous commitment it needs—often because we are overwhelmed with things like student loans. Saving a fifth of what you make may not be realistic, but taking on some side jobs is almost *always* preferable to saving little to nothing. Everyone needs to structure their budgets with basic savings and security as the top priority, even before debt repayment. An emergency fund is *nonnegotiable*, even if you have a million dollars of debt (living without an emergency fund is like driving without a seat belt).

And no matter how you decide to allocate your savings, debt repayment, and investment, the point is that you always do it with

Future You in mind: make sure that you are getting the absolute maximum benefit from each dollar in your budget (once you are finished saving up your emergency fund, of course). A good, long-term-oriented budget is the bedrock of your flexibility throughout life. Trust me, I have been on both sides, and it's much better with one than without.

At TFD, we also believe that budgets can and should be beautiful. You should have a method to track a month of spending that actually makes you want to do it and gives you something nice to look at in the process. In the same way that a lovely notebook makes you want to take notes during a meeting, imbuing your budget with some aesthetics will take some of the sting out of doing it. We believe firmly that a good budget should be hung on a wall or over a desk, along with things like day planners and calendars and to-do lists. Money isn't something to be kept in private hiding places; it should be something you look at every day to remind you of what you actually want and the progress you've made so far.

"When you start out as a bit of a hot mess (which we all are, at some point), you need to take baby steps to become really good with money."

When we started pursuing TFD full-time, it became clear early on that—especially when it comes to things like daily budgeting—every money expert has a different philosophy. There are some people who are radical debt-payers, others who focus heavily on investment, some who espouse super-minimalist lifestyles, some who vaunt the side hustle way more than paring down how you live. And it's difficult to say, when faced with the ever-expanding marketplace of financial ideas, which is the right path for you. It depends on a lot of different factors (everything from how much debt you have to how much you like to eat at restaurants), but we should all be able to be honest with ourselves about what we can stick to and accept that no one solution is going to work for everyone. We think that the only way to stay sane financially—unless you're planning on going on a really hard-core money lifestyle change (and there are a lot of personal finance plans that are, like, the CrossFit of money)—is to create your own collage of strategies that work for you.

Three of the money experts we follow have become friends and collaborators with TFD and have taught us a great deal about both personal finance and how to make money a more balanced part of your life. We spoke to all three about how they personally budget, how they approach finance, and the strategies that have helped them find the financial harmony they enjoy today.

Cait FLANDERS

Author, Cohost of
Budgets & Cents **Podcast**

Q. What are the three most important financial strategies you live by?

1. Pause before making any purchase. Whenever I think about making an impulse purchase, I stop and ask myself a few questions. First, what triggered it? Second, what's the environment like that I'm in? And finally, what story am I telling myself? If I am convincing myself I need to buy something, I put it down and walk away.

2. Live on as little as possible, then save the rest. I used to follow the standard advice offered by most personal finance experts, which is to save a percentage of your income first and then spend the rest. But the big problem with that is it gives you permission to spend a lot of money you could probably be saving. Now, I give myself the same (smaller) budget each month, and then save everything extra. This way, my spending doesn't fluctuate, but my savings potential is much greater.

3. Trust your gut. I know this isn't your typical financial advice, but hear me out. In my experience, whenever I used to swipe for something I couldn't afford, my body warned me. There was always a little feeling somewhere between my head and my heart that said, "You're adding to your debt," but I ignored it. Ignoring my gut instinct over and over again eventually resulted in my being maxed out with close to $30,000 of debt. Now, if my gut instinct is to spend less and save more, I listen.

Q. Can you give us a weeklong sample budget?

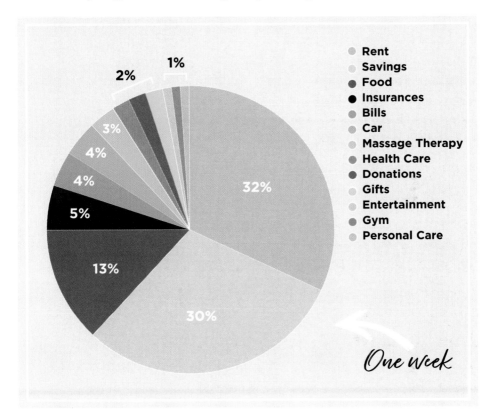

One week

Legend:
- Rent
- Savings
- Food
- Insurances
- Bills
- Car
- Massage Therapy
- Health Care
- Donations
- Gifts
- Entertainment
- Gym
- Personal Care

Pie chart values: 32%, 30%, 13%, 5%, 4%, 4%, 3%, 2%, 1%

And I might buy clothes twice a year, and spend no more than a few hundred dollars total.

> "In my experience, whenever I used to swipe for something I couldn't afford, my body warned me. There was always a little feeling somewhere between my head and my heart that said, 'You're adding to your debt,' but I ignored it."

J. MONEY

Founder of Award-Winning Finance Blogs *Budgets Are Sexy* and *Rockstar Finance*
Net worth $650,000

What are the three most important financial strategies you live by?

1. I strive for financial freedom instead of trying to be rich for the hell of it. Money is nice, but there has to be a point to it or you'll never have enough, ya know? And what's better than being able to do whatever you want every day?

2. I only work on stuff that "excites" me. I can't get motivated if I'm not super passionate about something, so as long as my actions are going toward improving my finances as a whole, I go for it. Even if it's not in the "right order," say, like paying off debt before investing. I'm also not afraid to change my mind and switch course since nothing in life is ever permanent!

3. I max out both my SEP IRA (I'm self-employed) as well as my Roth IRA every year [IRAs are non-employer-backed retirement accounts—you get them yourself]. It's not always the easiest, but by doing that alone you can't help but become a millionaire over time. It's simply a matter of harnessing the most powerful ingredient we have with our money— time!

Can you give us a weeklong sample budget?

Sure, here's how we roughly spend each week:

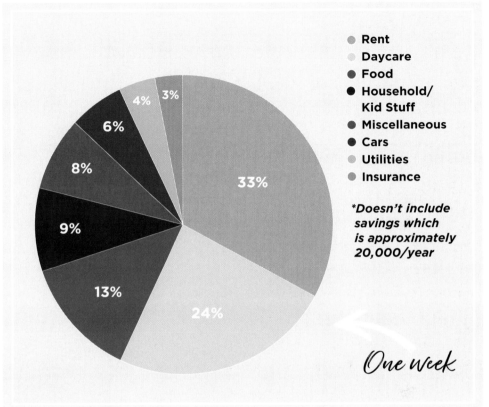

Legend:
- Rent
- Daycare
- Food
- Household/Kid Stuff
- Miscellaneous
- Cars
- Utilities
- Insurance

Doesn't include savings which is approximately 20,000/year

Pie chart values: 33%, 24%, 13%, 9%, 8%, 6%, 4%, 3%

One week

Can you talk about the value of tracking net worth, and the role it plays in your life?

Oh man, tracking my net worth was one of the best things I have ever done with my money! I use a spreadsheet where I track all my assets (savings, investments, cars), as well as my liabilities (car loan) and then the difference is my net worth. It's hard to track your progress if you don't have a clear understanding of where everything is (savings, investments, debts!), so spending 5 minutes a month updating that financial snapshot does wonders for accountability. I can't stress enough how much of a game changer this is. Do this one thing and it'll completely change how you look at your money, and your life, going forward.

What's been the most valuable financial challenge you've ever taken? How did it change your views on and about money?

Last year I decided to challenge all my expenses and see if I could maintain my same lifestyle, but pay less for it. I never thought I'd ever get rid of my iPhone or even cable, for that matter, but after really thinking about what I needed out of life, I cut down all the "extras" with the cable bill (eventually nixing it altogether), switched cell phone providers, saving me $100+/mo, lowered car insurance by changing deductibles and nixing add-ons, started selling one thing off Craigslist a week, thereby reducing clutter at the same time, and just became more conscious of *where* my money was going and *why*. Which made me realize two things:

a) Focusing your effort on recurring bills vs. one-off purchases gives you much more bang for your buck since the savings continue to roll in each month!

b) There are plenty of alternatives you can take advantage of that give you the same level of happiness but cost much less. When you realize that the less you need to live off every month, the less you need to make, it changes your perspective on everything. And technology is making this easier and easier as time goes on.

"Money is nice,
but there has to be
a point to it or you'll
never have enough."

Bridget CASEY

Finance MBA & Award-Winning Entrepreneur

Q. What are the three most important financial strategies you live by?

1. Your ability to cut expenses is limited; your earning potential is not. It is far easier to earn more money than it is to keep cutting back. Focus your efforts accordingly.

2. Reduce the number of decisions you have to make about your money by automating as much of it as you can. Schedule all your bill payments and savings transfers to coincide with payday, so everything you need to do happens on autopilot.

3. Always budget for a little bit of money for fun. No matter how big your debt or your financial goals are, you need some money you can spend guilt free to enjoy life in the present.

Q. Can you give us a weeklong sample budget?

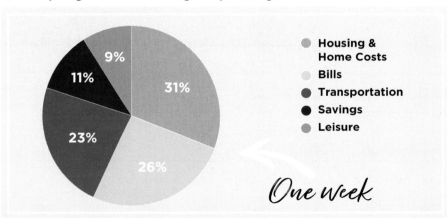

Housing & Home Costs — 31%
Bills — 26%
Transportation — 23%
Savings — 11%
Leisure — 9%

One week

I realize that's not what most people can or want to have, so what I typically suggest to people trying to make a budget is:

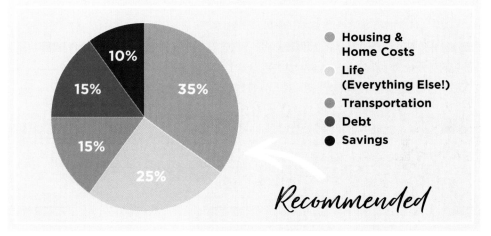

- Housing & Home Costs
- Life (Everything Else!)
- Transportation
- Debt
- Savings

35% 25% 15% 15% 10%

Recommended

Q. What percent of your total income do you invest (apart from basic savings)?

I invest 20 to 25% in a mix of stocks, ETFs, and mutual funds [different types of investment accounts that bundle a bunch of different stocks together]. I have an MBA in Finance so investing is my jam.

Q. What questions would you suggest someone ask themselves before they start investing?

The most important question is: How much work do you personally want to do when it comes to managing your investments? There's no right answer to this question, it's entirely personal preference. Some people really like to read quarterly stock reports and manage their own portfolio. Others simply want their money to be taken care of without having to worry about it, and a robo-advisor is the best fit for them. The second most important question is: What is your primary objective for investing? For some people it's growing their wealth, others want to generate passive income, some people want both. Knowing what you want to get out of investing determines what investments you choose.

When it comes to building your own perfect budget, as you can see, everyone is going to have a different strategy. It depends on what you need, what you want, and what you have. But there are good questions you can ask yourself to help decide what is the right path and structure for your money. Here is our cheat-sheet questionnaire, which will help you analyze your spending and savings.

Downloadable
RESOURCE

Budgeting Questions

1. What are three purchases I made last month that were impulsive?

2. How many of the purchases I made last month have long-term value?

3. What are three specific things I want to cut from my budget this month?

4. Of all the items I bought recently, have any of them gone on sale since?

5. How much money did I spend eating out last month?

6. Did I set a concrete savings goal, and did I meet it?

7. Going forward, what (specifically) am I saving up for?

8. How much do I need to save per week to meet that goal?

9. What is one tangible way I can increase my income next month?

10. Did I put money toward something I genuinely care about (e.g.—a memorable experience or a good cause)?

Visit
TheFinancialDiet.com/BookResources to Download

This isn't your foundational budget document, but it is designed to give you a financial snapshot and to inspire you to stay focused on your fiscal goals.

If you want to get good with money, the absolute first thing you need is a good budget. Period. Though we can't promise you that it will be the most fun thing you'll ever do (it won't), we can promise that it will have *the* biggest return on investment (a little money humor for everyone!). For the price of zero dollars and a few hours, you'll be asking yourself the questions and putting together the framework that will let you take control of your day-to-day life for the rest of your life. Nothing feels more badass than having that control, and knowing where your money is coming from and going to each month. And nothing feels more adult than being able to plan for a real future that looks like what you want it to look like.

Chapter 2

How to Be Your Money's Asshole Boss

Waiting until you're rich to start caring about your money is like waiting until you're married to start dating.

When I was growing up, my family always had a very large round wooden dining table. They had this table not because it was the most convenient way for four people to eat dinner—it definitely wasn't—but because it was the best table to host their famous poker parties. As a little kid, poker parties meant that I got to stay up as late as I wanted watching movies in my parents' bedroom, snacking on all the delicious finger foods my mom made for the guests. (I'd also usually wrangle a few bags of candy out of the deal, if I promised to keep my little sister from leaving the bedroom.) And as I got older, I was allowed to spend increasingly long stretches of time at the table with the grown-ups, learning the game and making them laugh, so as not to wear out my welcome. By the time I was twenty-one, and coming home for holidays, I could sit at the table for an entire evening, sipping a vodka soda and playing poker with men more than twice my age. There was something incredibly special to me about being able to play a real game, to bet my $15 or so and spend the night listening to stories, and telling a few of my own occasionally. In many ways, I measured my adulthood against my role in those poker games—and betting (and potentially winning) money was a big part of what made it feel thrilling. For the longest time, I looked at the idea of investment the way I looked at poker: it was largely the domain of older men who knew what they were doing in a way I did not, and it almost always ended in me losing the money.

It really wasn't until I started TFD, and began to learn the basics of investing, that I started to believe having a "diversified portfolio" was something I could achieve. For example, that 401(k) letter from HR at my old job I'd promptly thrown in the trash? That actually meant something. If I'd taken advantage of it, I'd have several thousand extra dollars right now, which would be accruing more money while it sat in that account. But I didn't know what the term "401(k)" even meant, and I was too lazy to ask. I couldn't understand why I'd spend an hour setting up an account so my money could sit somewhere instead of it being liquidated at a happy hour. It didn't make sense to me that "investment" could mean something slow and steady like that—or that it could be as simple as an hour with my HR person.

Of course, investment is nothing like poker, unless you do it like an enormous idiot. Point-blank, investing is neither scary nor difficult. You have to know a few basic rules, and get fluent in a few strategies, but it's something everyone can master—even with just a few extra dollars a month. And we would never encourage you to become like those middle-aged dudes who suddenly become borderline hermits and spend eighty hours a week "day trading" in their underwear. But, one of the most important parts of understanding investment is to start young: it's easy to feel like the "making your money work" bullshit only applies to old people with a lot of money, but let me tell you, it very much does not. Being young is like having a secret cheat code to increasing your wealth, because your money has a much longer time to grow.

Giving yourself the right vocabulary—check our glossary at the back for tons of useful investment terms—and understanding the basic underlying principles of investing are half the battle. Most of us avoid thinking about our money in terms of investment because it feels confusing or unnecessarily complicated. We can often visualize investment as this extremely active process, something that needs to be your full-time job to truly master. But there are hundreds of ways to go about it, and because many of them are passive, are simple to set up, and require very little amounts of money, an entire world opens up to you. You don't have to be some stock photo of a money manager holding sacks of dollar bills to invest. You can do it in a few hours by setting something up with your HR department. Hell, even paying down your debt is an investment in your financial future.

It's important that you start looking at your money like it's the

The Total Idiot's Guide to Investing

1. Save an emergency fund of at least three months' worth of living costs.

2. Pay down your debt by creating a debt repayment schedule that minimizes interest and maximizes benefit. (Compare the interest you're accruing on your debt to the return on investment for a dollar amount per month, accounting for taxes. Where will your dollar do more work?)

3. Open a retirement account, ideally with an employer match, like a 401(k). Make sure to maximize what your employer matches, if you have an employer match available on your 401(k).

4. Explore other low-risk investment options, such as mutual funds and index funds.

5. After you've done all this, you can consider individual stocks if you feel confident in your investing savvy and feel strongly about the companies you're investing in. (This is what a lot of people think of when they visualize "investing," but it's far from the only way, and it's not at all necessary to invest in individual stocks to be an investor—in fact, many people don't because it carries a much higher risk!)

asshole boss: it shouldn't just sit there in some boring account, doing nothing (except for your emergency fund, which is boring but absolutely necessary). Your money should be actively working, and always doing something that is to your benefit, and always reaching toward a goal on its own. The best part is that doing this doesn't even require a dangerous, risky, and complex strategy that's way too complicated for you to understand. And if I can figure it out, trust me, so can you. But you have to know where to start.

One thing that is essential to understand, when it comes to investment, is that a dollar in your budget is not necessarily just a dollar. Yes, a dollar could be something you choose to spend on a couch or a shirt or coffee, but if and when we have the opportunity—because, yes, sometimes we simply don't have the money to invest—investing makes that one dollar worth potentially much, much more. To not take advantage of, at the very least, a basic retirement account and the interest over time we stand to gain from it is to shoot ourselves in the foot (or bank account).

I won't oversell it and promise you that you are going to be a millionaire by the time you are fifty if you put a penny in some account every day, but we all have the opportunity to accrue wealth if we start investing young. We all have the opportunity to be one of those people with a real nest egg, a real retirement plan, and a real inheritance to pass down. And figuring out the value of an investment is a lot easier than you think. In fact, there is a simple, straightforward rule that allows you to quickly calculate compound interest, which will allow you to visualize the long-term potential of an investment, see how much fees and charges might really amount to over the years, and decide among different options. Master the rule of 72, and you'll quickly become a wizard at analyzing a lot of these tricky numbers.

RULE OF 72:

A simple rule to determine how long an investment will take to double. Simply divide the number 72 by your compound annual interest rate. (And remember, a rate of 5 percent would be expressed as 5, not .05.)

Now, these are the basic things that you should understand, and they are huge in helping to get you on the road of investment. But when you are just getting started with making your money work, you will probably need some help. You may already be able to speak some of the investing language, but in order to become fluent, you will need to find a financial Sherpa. When you're starting from zero, there are going to be so many things that you don't even know you don't know, and chances will be high that even simple terms will be outside your realm of knowledge. (When I began, I didn't know what a stock was, to give some sense of where I was.) Finding someone you trust to help you learn the basics, as well as give you some sage advice, is of the utmost importance. Even with all the wonderful information available to you on Ye Olde Google, if you don't know the questions you should be asking, it can be tough to make headway. Now, this Sherpa could be anyone from a professional money manager to a trustworthy member of your own family who has experience investing. Ideally, you want to go in with at least some vague goals in mind, and having done enough basic research so that you can start a conversation, which is the first step toward meeting those goals.

One of those first financial Sherpas will often be your own HR person, who is there to help you learn about the retirement accounts, which should be your first stop when it comes to investing. Retirement accounts are one of the safest, easiest-to-start types of investments, requiring little involvement on your part, and whether you plan to have a complex portfolio beyond that, or simply stop with your most basic 401(k), a retirement account is a nonnegotiable. And that goes double when your employer is matching your contributions. All of the basic types of retirement accounts—like 401(k)s, IRAs, or Roth IRAs—are easily available and quite simple to set up. And depending on the account type, they can come with huge benefits. To explain everything we need to know about navigating retirement accounts, I brought in the dream HR person you wish you had at your office to help you, Kristen Robinson. Kristen is senior vice president of emerging investors at Fidelity, whose actual day job is "helping young women get good with money and get over their fear of scary investing terms."

Here's what she had to say about the often-intimidating world of retirement accounts:

Refer to the glossary on page 188 to learn the difference between basic types of investment, from stocks and bonds to ETFs and index funds.

Kristen ROBINSON

SVP of Emerging Investors at Fidelity

Q: Can you explain what an IRA and Roth IRA are, and how they are different from a 401(k)? Are there other retirement accounts people should know about?

A: IRAs and Roth IRAs are both retirement savings accounts that you can open as an individual. A 401(k) is a retirement savings account that is sponsored by your employer. The rules on how much you can contribute and how much is tax-deductible or tax-deferred varies by account type. For 401(k)s, the employer match allows employers to match contributions to the 401(k) up to a certain percentage. As a general rule, once you've contributed the full amount to your 401(k) that will allow you to receive the maximum employer match offered, you could consider supplementing that by opening an IRA or another tax-advantaged retirement savings vehicle.

Although investing in a 401(k) does have advantages (which can include certain tax advantages, creditor protection, and possibly lower fees), one benefit to contributing to an IRA is that it gives you access to a wide range of investments, often more extensive than 401(k)s, including stocks, bonds, mutual funds, and ETFs. IRAs come in different varieties, such as the "traditional" IRA and Roth IRAs. Although both allow you to set aside up to $5,500 each year ($6,500 if you are fifty or older), they have different advantages.

In a traditional IRA, you make contributions with money you may be able to deduct on your tax return and any earnings can potentially grow, tax-deferred, until you withdraw them in retirement. With a Roth IRA, you make contributions with money you've already paid taxes on (after-tax) and your money may potentially grow tax-free, with tax-free withdrawals in retirement, provided that certain conditions are met.

There are also other retirement accounts people should be aware of. Spousal IRAs—for "stay-at-home" spouses—can help couples with one income earner get the same amount of tax-advantaged IRA savings opportunities as couples in which both earn income. There are certain qualifications and limits: you must be married and file a joint tax return in the years you plan to contribute. Since all IRA contributions must come from earned income, you would make contributions for your spouse from your wages. Setting up a spousal IRA is fairly easy. All your spouse would need to do is to open a traditional or Roth IRA and then contributions could be made to that account.

There are even Roth IRAs for kids. Even if you are a minor, you can start saving for your future retirement. As long as you have earned income, you can make a contribution to a Roth IRA for kids, though certain restrictions do apply.

And finally, there's something called a catch-up contribution. Those age fifty or older have the ability to make additional contributions to their IRAs and 401(k)s when they turn fifty. This additional amount can potentially help them increase their retirement savings.

Q: Is there a situation in which someone should use more than one?

A: Yes, it is quite common to make contributions to both a 401(k) and an IRA each year. While the 401(k) would be funded with pre-tax contributions from your paycheck, the IRA would be funded with contributions from your own money (that is, from your bank account). There are limits for both, as well as tax deductibility and eligibility issues for traditional IRA and Roth IRA contributions. People can also have a 401(k) or other workplace-sponsored retirement plan account and also a small business account for an unaffiliated business they might have on the side.

Q: If someone doesn't have access to a retirement account through work or is self-employed, what is their best similar option?

A: If someone doesn't have access to a 401(k) at work or other such workplace-sponsored account, they can consider a traditional or Roth IRA as their first investing option. However, if someone is self-employed, there are some additional options to consider. These include:

SEP IRAs: Designed for a self-employed individual or small business owner, including those with employees. This is funded solely by employer contributions and allows employers to contribute up to 25 percent of compensation up to a maximum of $53,000.

Self-Employed 401(k)s: Designed for a self-employed individual or business owner with no employees other than a spouse. This is funded by employee deferrals of up to $18,000 ($24,000 if fifty or older) and employer contributions of up to 25 percent of compensation up to a maximum of $53,000.

SIMPLE IRAs: (savings incentive match plan for employees individual retirement accounts): Designed for businesses with one hundred or fewer employees and self-employed individuals. This is also funded by employee deferrals of up to $12,500 ($15,500 if fifty or older) and employer contributions up to a maximum of $5,300.

Q: What are the biggest things that a young, newly professional woman should know about retirement accounts in general?

A: With time on your side, saving even a little more today can mean a lot more money in your pocket in the long run. Challenge yourself to skip one restaurant lunch or dinner a month and increase the percentage of your paycheck that you put into your retirement savings account. Simple trade-offs that really aren't a sacrifice can help put our money to work for us and have a big impact in the future.

Always take advantage of "free money" at your job. If you're saving in a workplace retirement account but not meeting the company match, you're missing out on free money. For many, there is a missed learning opportunity at many workplaces, too: among women who are offered retirement guidance through their employer, 65 percent do not take advantage of it. It's okay that you don't have all the answers, but it's important to make sure the money you're working hard to save is also working hard for you. Retirement savings accounts offer a range of investment options—from conservative to aggressive, depending on your goals, the time you have to save and invest, and your comfort level with fluctuations in the market. Need help determining the best investment mix for your individual goals? There are plenty of resources available to help.

So ask for help—it's available everywhere! And know that you don't have to pay for financial advice. Don't hesitate to take advantage of free financial workshops or one-on-one guidance offered at your workplace, or reach out directly to firms like Fidelity that are happy to talk to you on the phone, online, or in person at a branch—at no cost, no strings attached.

Once you've got your retirement account squared away and working to turn your money acorns into eventual money oak trees, it's time to think about investment in a more macro sense. Now, by no means do you *have* to invest beyond a retirement account (at least not right away). But if you are interested in taking a more active role in your money in the long term and in having diverse assets—everything from home(s) to individual stocks to bigger funds are ways to make your money work—you should know the basic playbook of investing. I promise, you don't have to become some *Wolf of Wall Street* parody to make the most of your money. And there is nothing stopping you from planting the seeds now, even just a few dollars a month.

But don't take it from me. Take it from someone who actually lived (and left) the Wall Street life and now runs a school that is based on being smart with money without it becoming your whole life. Jane Hwangbo, founder of Money School with Jane, puts that evil face of investing—the money-hungry, eighties-movie version we often associate with stockbrokers in bad suits—this way:

"Investing on Wall Street is about winning, as purely competitive as professional athletics. Besting your peers is the only game worth playing. You get to stay if you keep beating your opponents, and you're only as good as your last score. On the Street, the goal of winning must be met, every day of every year. You can never stop. When I joined one of the most respected and largest technology-focused hedge funds in the nineties as a semiconductor analyst, I was one of those winners. I thought I was going to make a ton of money and be really happy. I was wrong on one count.

"I didn't realize that Wall Street's investing style is like having sex without love, over and over again. After a while, you burn out. I was becoming the most uninteresting person I knew. My personality had compressed to the width of a cardboard sheet, and I was starved for purpose."

The first night we met Jane, over a few good martinis, she explained how that life—money for money's sake, competition for competition's sake—burned her out and left her facing serious existential and personal crises. She told us about how much she worried that people interested in investing "seriously"—even people who wanted to do it from the comfort of their own homes, for just their own purposes—might approach the world of investment with this same unhealthy, gamelike mentality. While many people might shy away from ever "making their money work," feeling unqualified or baffled by the system, the people who pursued it might just follow the same patterns the Wall Street culture put in place, albeit on a smaller scale. She reminded us repeatedly how much one's money life must be balanced and based on human goals, not numerical ones.

That theory of sustainability—taking the best of investment culture and making something human out of it—is what drives Jane today. She has created a way of thinking about investing for the average young woman, so we can all make our money work like our asshole bosses without risking our emergency funds or our souls.

Jane HWANGBO

Founder of *Money School with Jane*

10 Investing Rules Every Woman Should Follow

1. Money is a tool, not a goal. When you're clear about this, you'll make a million small financial decisions differently, enabling you to better work toward reaching your bigger goals. Take some time to define what you personally want to do with your money in the future.

2. Amass an SOS fund. Before you even think about investing, you need to have an emergency fund of at least six months' worth, tucked away in an untouchable cash account that you've mentally labeled as your Save Our Souls account. Investing without a healthy cash reserve is similar to driving a race car without a seat belt. Smart people don't do it.

3. Become numerate and learn basic financial terminology. Move beyond memorizing words and practice contextualizing terms within a financial story. All assets (stocks, bonds, real estate, or partnership interests) have a financial story. As an investor, you'll need to define the stories and validate whether they make sense.

4. Get comfortable with basic accounting and get used to working with numbers. Know how to assess the three tells of a productive asset: the income statement, balance sheet, and cash flow statement. The keenness you gain from this eye-rolling hard work will pay off for years in returns. It will change the way you look at any stock, bond, piece of investment property, or even index ETF. Those who put in the work reap the rewards.

5. Open retirement accounts first: 401(k)s, Roth IRAs, and traditional IRAs.

"Free-limited-time-offer-only" money gets invested first, followed by tax-deferred funds, and then fully taxable funds. Translation: take advantage of employer-matching 401(k) programs that literally offer you free, pre-tax money. Since investment money compounds, any additional small boosts of funding at the start can make a big difference over the long run.

6. Where possible, build your passive investment income stream next. Focus on building a portfolio of investments that allow for a regular, passive income ("passive" meaning requiring limited day-to-day management by you) that can support your desired lifestyle, regardless of what happens in your career. It's a lofty goal, but you're truly wealthy when your investments can fund your living expenses and you are no longer dependent on your salary or wages.

7. Forget the traditional rules of asset allocation and invest according to what you know about your own personality. The best investments will be the ones you can live with in terms of risk and reward. This requires really getting comfortable with who you are. You don't need to invest in aggressive equities just because you're young. You can buy bonds, reinvest, and do very, very well. Conversely, you don't have to buy bonds when you're older if you've already created a solid stream of passive income from previous investments.

8. When investing in a business, properly assess its financial strategy. In other words, figure out how a business can make a sustainable profit one day, not just sales, so that as an investor, you can receive returns through either cash distributions or dividends.

9. Don't take your investment failures personally. Investments are probabilistic bets in nature, not sure things. The best investors know this and try to learn from the choices they made that didn't work out. Facts also change. Reevaluate your assumptions and be aware of your own behavioral biases.

10. Be patient. Investing will test you, wear you out, make you grow, and change you. Trust in the process, and make your big decisions based on the long term. You'll need to stay true to your vision in order to realize it.

Investing is scary. There's no arguing that. But there is an intelligent, balanced way to approach investment that helps you reach your goals in a passive, low-impact way—one that makes the money that was otherwise just sitting there into a new stream of income. Even if your first step is simply e-mailing an HR person to ask a few basic questions, it's just important that you start. There is no magic key that makes someone "an investor" or "not an investor": the information is available to all of us. We can all decide the kind of portfolio we'd like to have, and the future we want it to create for ourselves—as long as we ask questions and pay close attention to the answers. Inform yourself, come armed with the goals you want to achieve and how you're comfortable with achieving them, and get started.

It doesn't matter if it's just a few dollars a day; the point is it isn't nothing. You can be one of those people who uses words like "portfolio," and you don't have to be a monster to get there. You can just be you, except smarter with your money.

Chapter 3

How to Be the CEO of Your Life

If you're going to have to work, you might as well do it right.

I have been fired from approximately a dozen jobs in my life. And I say approximately not because I'm trying to fudge the numbers but rather because I simply lost track at a certain point. There was a period in my life—roughly fifteen to twenty-two—where I treated my professional life as a series of bridges to be burned. I hopped around to a new city, and then a new country, to find a place where my budding professional reputation wasn't somewhere between "unwieldy but talented" and "legal liability who should be escorted out by security." It was easy for me to be constantly running to the next company that would take me, because I never took myself seriously. I was once fired at twenty-one from an upscale coffee shop because I called to get out of a shift at 4:45 a.m. still drunk after a David Guetta concert. I viewed the concept of having a capital-C Career as both unreasonable and undesirable.

But, as you may have guessed, my worldview has changed. I have a small but growing company that needs me. I love my professional life in a way that I never considered possible because I've realized that how I treat my work is a huge part of who I am as a person. I've also come to understand that my job is not my defining feature. My old fears of "becoming a boring Company Woman" and "even slightly compromising my social life for a job" now seem ridiculous because balance is (usually) achievable. Now, despite putting considerably more effort into my career than I ever had before, I find myself with more (and more enjoyable) free time. I have learned to prioritize the things I need to get done and those that I can put off, and so my evenings out aren't spent in a state of mild panic over all the things I didn't do or the lies I told my boss to get out of a task. There is a powerful calm that comes from taking yourself seriously.

I—and I think a lot of other people—assumed that I would eventually find the magic job that would make me the person I wanted to be. But the truth is that we should approach each job the same way:

by bringing our A game. After you've developed your work ethic, you have to figure out how to find fulfillment in your work and to decide what is actually important to you in a career. Even the most type A list maker can easily find herself having made all the right choices and hate where they led her. And worse, our expectations about what the "right" job will look like can often set us up for disappointment. Figuring out how to make the most of what we have or admitting we want to change paths can often be even harder than securing a career in the first place.

For many of us, the life we might imagine for ourselves is simply out of reach or leaves us with no clear road map to get there. Even when we're able to be lucid about what we want professionally, we may be dealing with a monthly budget that won't let us make those moves. Every day at TFD, we hear from young women who hate their well-paying jobs but have zero chance of leaving them in the next several years because those same jobs are the only thing allowing them to make their loan payments each month without having to Airbnb out their bedroom while they live in their shower. And even in that unfortunate situation, there is still a huge amount of privilege: there are so many people who are dealing with a) jobs they hate that b) pay absolute shit, and c) they need those jobs to pay their sky-high monthly bills.

And this is why getting your financial situation in order is so important. Unless you have an iron grip on your budget, know what you're spending and why, and have explored every possible avenue to diversify your revenue and money growth, you can't expect to have much professional freedom. You have to have financial stability to pursue your professional dreams—this means being brutally honest about your spending habits and lifestyle, and deciding where you can cut to make room for a little more flexibility and time. Point-blank, the more control you have over your financial destiny, the more control you'll have over your professional path. Saving, living below your means, and diversifying your income often make the difference between being stuck in a job you can't stand and having the freedom to move on to something better.

Having a career that is both fulfilling and successful also means deciding who you want to be and working on becoming that person in more than just your e-mail strategy: What time do you want to wake up? How do you want to look walking into an office? How good do you want to be at things like networking or public speaking? Embodying your professional selves outside the office means forcing yourself to take your habits as seriously as you do your deadlines.

One of the most useful and liberating pieces of advice I ever received was: "Put a value on your time, and start measuring your wealth not in money but in freedom." Ever since, I've been thinking in terms of the value I get out of an hour spent, and how I can maximize that value per hour so that I get more done in a smaller amount of time and still have more freedom to pursue both the things I love and the things that help me grow within the context of my professional life. Hobbies, classes, learning new skills, taking on side jobs: these are all essential components of a fulfilled life, but they can so easily get trimmed from the to-do list if we start prioritizing only the things that immediately make us the most money. Ultimately, a job, no matter how much you love it, will never hit every note for you, and it shouldn't. We should all strive to find multiple streams of fulfillment, challenges, and income. The more we rely on one role as an all-encompassing definition, the unhealthier our relationship with that role becomes.

I'm a huge advocate of the side hustle, and not just because it allows you to reach your financial goals. It's also wonderful, in general, to have a few other things to focus on and give yourself to, things that perhaps demand and grow different skills and remind you

"Put a value on your time, and start measuring your wealth not in money but in freedom."

that there is a whole goddamn life outside the horizons of your main job.

When I was younger, I was fucking up at my jobs so badly because I was only looking at my life in the short term and refusing to think or plan for Future Chelsea. I wanted to take the quickest and most painless way out every time, which only compounded my problems and limited my choices in the long term. And there are still many times when I face down these impulses—when I choose to watch more TV instead of going to that interesting-sounding workshop, or allow my laziness to turn what should be a two-hour task into a two-day one.

In writing this chapter, I spoke to brilliant, badass women who are career experts, but not in the "How to Become a CEO by Ruthlessly Murdering Your Work–Life Balance" way. The TFD view on work has always been "lean in sometimes, but also lean the hell out other times, because you're a human and humans should be defined by way more than their job title," and these women embody it. I talked to these amazing women about how to actually define what a career means, how to create one on your own terms, and how to get your finances in the right place to make attainable some of the bigger dreams you have. I even talked to them about creating the personal style that will get you closer to the professional you that you want to be. Ultimately, we are all the CEOs of our own lives, and that means every hour should be accounted for and well compensated, according to our own personal standards of wealth and happiness.

One of the most meaningful differences, professionally speaking, between Chelsea of Today and hot mess Chelsea has to do with finding and keeping good mentors. And chief among the women I'm lucky enough to consider as a mentor is Joanne Cleaver. Joanne is a business journalist, author, consultant, and entrepreneur with decades of experience and a dizzying passion for helping women in the working world. She found TFD in its infancy and wrote a magazine feature on the site, asking us to pitch ourselves when we barely knew what that pitch was. She took us to symposiums and functions and introduced us to women who have been doing decades of hard work advocating for women in the workplace and giving them the financial tools for independence. Joanne showed us, early on, that there is a life's work to be found in making finance and professional literacy something all women can participate in.

Joanne CLEAVER

**Business Journalist, Author
Consultant, and Entrepreneur**

If you want to be "successful" in your career today, your first step will be getting over the old definitions of success: career paths are morphing much more quickly than the language that describes them. That's why you still read articles about "climbing the ladder" when that ladder has all but disappeared. Defining career success in three dimensions—up, over, and, occasionally, out—opens up a fresh spectrum of opportunities. But you still have to get a foothold and gain traction.

Networking within a company or industry is a secret weapon for scoping out potential opportunities and for developing relationships that convert to referrals. Your goal is both to be known by the right people and to be known for the right things. So how do you do that? Not with your boss. She has her hands full with getting you and your teammates to achieve the team's official goals. (Never forget that one of the most important ways you can build your reputation is to make your boss look good. That means understanding what incentives are built into her bonus and how you can make her look good to *her* boss.)

Here are six proven strategies for quickly building a network within your company and your industry. Even if you decide you want to switch jobs, it's a lot easier to find one within your current industry than it is to start all over in a different industry.

1. Volunteer.

That's right: work for free. If it makes it easier, think of it as working for yourself, with a payoff to come. I used this strategy when I was a deputy business and real estate editor at a city newspaper. Everybody in the newsroom hated the annual United Way charity drive. People in the newsroom loved to complain about all the problems in our city, but they largely refused to write checks to solve those problems, even though our president was on the regional United Way board.

I connived with a couple of newsroom friends to create a mock newspaper that reproduced some of the most heartrending stories we'd recently published and stories about how giving would address those problems. I also went full-on homemaker with a fancy bake sale and cupcake competition. The strategies worked: the newsroom donated more than it ever had before.

A couple of weeks later, I was summoned to a meeting in the executive suite. When I arrived, my immediate boss and his immediate boss were waiting for me. So was the president. It turned out that the president loved the mock newspaper so much that she brought a stack of them to the next United Way meeting to show all the other big shots. Taking on a thankless task built my reputation with the top honcho and down the food chain.

2. Find ways to work alongside company and industry influencers.

A staffer at a Washington, D.C., nonprofit was having trouble finding a good fit in the sprawling world of nonprofits in the Washington, D.C., area. There's tons of competition for nonprofit jobs. She didn't want to wait her turn forever.

How could she meet executive directors who were in a position to refer her to the kinds of jobs she wanted? By volunteering alongside them at events they cared about personally. She researched volunteer boards through LinkedIn and detected a handful of causes that were led by influential women.

The right event opportunity came up and she pounced. The work was not glamorous: coming early, setting up, taking tickets, staying late to clean up. But she did these chores in the company of women executive directors who saw firsthand how this staffer worked, cheerfully and reliably. And she told them about her career ambitions. Not a week later, she received a call from one of the high-level volunteers, with a referral to the job that ultimately catapulted the staffer to executive director of a nonprofit.

3. Bring in customers and clients, no matter what your official job is.
Wait, you say: I'm not in sales! Yes, you are. Everybody is in sales. Thanks to the reach of social media, every staffer is in a position to introduce potential clients to the people within your company who'd have official responsibility for translating contacts to customers.

4. Professional empathy.
Possess the ability to listen and truly understand what the other person thinks she needs and what she actually needs. These are networking skills that you can cultivate no matter where you start and no matter where you work.

5. A mastery of (good) networking.
The rise of social media and the fall of traditional career paths have not changed one core truth: people like to work with people they know, trust, and like. Finding new career opportunities is about you. And it's about others. Networking is helping others help you.

6. Thinking outside your role.
Don't be afraid of doing something that isn't a concrete task in your preexisting job or something that doesn't seem to have an immediate benefit for you. Climbing the career lattice is all about laying the groundwork now for something much better down the road.

"Never forget that one of the most important ways you can build your reputation is to make your boss look good. That means understanding what incentives are built into her bonus and how you can make her look good to *her* boss."

Building your career is an ongoing, imperfect process, one that requires regular assessment of where you are. Even if you love your current job, current company, current industry, it's important that you ask yourself some key questions at least once a year, to decide if you're making the most of what you have, and in a role that is actually taking you where you want to go. It's not unhealthy or wrong to change your mind, career-wise, nor is it selfish to dream for something better than what you have, even if what you already have is "pretty good" compared to what other people have. You have to judge your career and success—financial and otherwise—based on you, and you alone. If you're not happy, change something.

And how do you know if you're not happy? By asking yourself some serious questions. And luckily for us, Joanne has created her annual Career Checkup, which gives us the questions we need to understand where we really are in our careers and what we want to change.

Joanne's
Career Checkup

7 Questions You Should Ask Yourself About Your Job Every Year

1. Am I cultivating at least two relationships within my industry (outside my company)?

2. Am I cultivating at least two relationships related to the skills I want to develop (inside my company or outside)?

3. What skills will I likely need to have to qualify for the job I would like in five years?

4. What experiences and success stories would I likely need to have to qualify for the job I would like to have in five years?

5. What teams/projects/committees am I on that expand my network outside my circle of daily coworkers and collaborators?

6. What industry leaders (companies) am I following to identify trends in the industry I want to be in?

7. What industry leaders (individuals) am I following to identify successful career strategies that I might adopt or adapt?

Visit
TheFinancialDiet.com/BookResources to Download

Making the most of our career paths within the confines of our primary job is hugely important, and if we're not all climbing the lattice (instead of waiting for a hot firefighter to pull us up the career ladder), we're making a huge mistake. But the work doesn't end there, financially or personally. Whether it's because you want to earn a little more money, have a little more diversity in your skill set, or possibly start a transition toward a new field, it's important that you master the Art of the Side Hustle. Finding the most painless and beneficial ways to add to your bottom line and hone a new skill are keys not just to freedom but to a certain amount of security. As my good friend and serial side hustler Stephanie Georgopulos puts it, "Having multiple streams of income doesn't just mean money, it means no one employer is your professional destiny."

Stephanie is someone who went from working at a hair salon, utterly broke and drowning in student debt, to building her dream career out of little bits and pieces over the course of six or so years. She did it through always having jobs, and side jobs, and side-side jobs, and constantly asking herself what she could do tomorrow that she didn't know how to do today. She gave me her biggest rules for having a good side-hustle game, no matter what your main job is.

Stephanie GEORGOPULOS

Serial Side Hustler

Q. Describe how you went from a hair salon to having a prestigious full-time media job.

After graduation I needed money ASAP, so I interviewed for a salon coordinator position. I was making $10 an hour with no benefits, but I did have a computer and time to kill. So I started blogging and found My Voice 1.0. As I accumulated an audience, I felt more confident approaching bloggers with bigger readerships and asking how I could contribute (for free). Then I began pitching actual publications. I was still writing for free, but I began to see a future and I was high on that. I decided to quit the salon on a whim after being syndicated on Gizmodo. Now jobless, I took on any gig that would supplement my writing—social media, focus groups, whatever. Writing-wise, I found paid work through Craigslist, then word of mouth, then I strong-armed my way into part-time work with a publication that would eventually hire me full-time. My second job came via a referral from a friend who'd been following my writing, and I took on a freelance role with my current company (Medium) that same month. I did both jobs simultaneously for two years until I was in the financial position to freelance full-time. But six months later, my Medium contract ended and I was back to scrapping. Then they posted a job opening that looked perfect for me, and because of our prior working relationship and a solid interview, I was green-lit to try out the role on a contract basis. I was hired full-time two months later.

Q. What is your overall theory/mantra when it comes to side hustles? Do you still have them now that you have an "ideal" job?

Check in with yourself. Challenge the sunk-cost fallacy: the belief that you can't walk away from something because you've invested too much time emotion/value already and you need to see it through. You don't. If a side hustle isn't as fun or lucrative as it was in the beginning (or in your imagination), walk away. Find the next project.

I'm not off the side-hustle market, but I'm a lot more selective now. I kind of Marie Kondo'ed my side hustles—I love my job and it's my first priority, and a lot of the projects I took on as a freelancer were either underpaid or tedious. I'd rather work on something that's mine for free than pocket an extra $100. I'm always open to the right project, though.

Q. What would you say to someone who feels too tired at the end of the day to do anything else?

There are legit reasons someone might need their post-work energy (like, keeping another human alive). But one thing I can suggest is looking for side hustles that don't use the same part of your brain as your job. If you're on a computer all day, you might want to try something physical or intuitive (I make and sell tinctures, for example). If you work in a corporate environment, babysitting might be an enjoyable contrast. Choose something that invigorates you and strengthens your skill set. And be honest about how you're budgeting your time—if you're shuffling through the happy-hour-to-hangover pipeline, of course you're gonna be tired at the end of the workday. Work–life balance is important, but I admittedly sacrificed a lot of early mornings and weekends to make the freelance/full-time thing work.

No matter what you do for work, though, you are almost guaranteed to constantly be falling behind if you do not get the highest level of compensation you can for your jobs—whether a full-time career or a one-off side gig, you need to be knowledgeable and confident about getting what you are worth. Negotiating for fair compensation is a skill that everyone has to learn in their own way, and it is always going to be scary at first, but the sooner you get used to demanding proper payment, the more money you will have in the long run. (You're doing the job anyway. Why not get the most money for it?)

How to Get Paid What You Deserve

#1.

Figure out what an appropriate/competitive salary is for your desired job. Consider things like your age, level of experience, location, and job type, and search on websites like Glassdoor and PayScale. You can also ask people who work in the industry already, by taking someone to a brain-picking lunch or even asking the Internet at large—forums like Reddit or even Yahoo! Answers are great resources to ask the Internet how much they make for a certain job, and you can do it anonymously!

#2.

Go in prepared to negotiate their opening offer, and remember that a) you can negotiate in things other than money (maybe you want to work from home one or two days a week?), and b) negotiation is the sign of a confident professional, not a brat. Never be ashamed to negotiate. Stay positive, take your time (you can always ask to be able to take some time to consider the offer—in fact, you *should* do this), and never be overly impressed with an initial offer. Even if it seems like a big number, keep your cool.

#3.

Whether for your starting salary or your fifth raise, DON'T compare yourself to coworkers, DON'T get personal, and DON'T threaten to leave. DO your research, DO provide details of your achievements, and DO practice what you want to say beforehand. Compensation should be based on you and your performance, not anyone else's.

#4.

Always demonstrate that you can execute the higher-level job you want *before* you angle for a promotion. The sad truth is, you have to over-perform at your current job to merit a better one, and even if you do, you sometimes may need to go to another company to get that position you want.

#5.

The best way to have a competitive salary is to start high. This means that staying at the same place for too long, even if you do get the promotions you want, might actually be hurting you. If your compensation feels behind what it could be, and a good offer comes along, don't let a sense of loyalty get in the way of doing what's right for your career. Considerately leaving a job is not an evil thing.

#6.

Invest in yourself and in building your career skills: take an online class, attend a workshop, or invite out someone senior in your industry for coffee or a meal. You want to become an asset to any company and command the salary you deserve, but the only way to stay agile and irreplaceable is to stay well informed and ahead of the curve. This means always updating your software, so to speak.

Once you have figured out your best strategies for getting ahead at your main job and have explored the whole carnival of options that exist *outside* your day job, it's time to start thinking about the person you want to be as you pursue these opportunities, that is, work–life balance. The busier I've gotten over the years, the clearer it's become to me that there are several habits in my life that were preventing me from getting ahead of my own to-do list, and leaving me constantly trembling and stressed, like an Italian greyhound tied up outside a coffee shop. There are two major things I do to help keep the "life" in work–life balance.

1. Find time to sleep.

I had to start forcing myself to sleep well and wake up earlier. I will never be a morning person, per se, but I did become the person who is in relative control of my sleeping patterns and who wakes up feeling pretty refreshed.

2. Switch off.

I'm the kind of person who thrives on social contact, but I wasn't participating in the limited time I had with the people I cared about, and it left me constantly feeling depleted and resentful. My solution? Start having sacred, off-line, phone- or laptop-less times with people. I force myself to be completely present when I'm with friends. Because if I don't make it a conscious effort, I'll never get out of my own brain, and those relationships that are most important to me suffer.

Up until I started TFD, really, I still dressed and carried myself like a kid. I thought of myself as being much younger than I was, and I felt awkward in meetings or presentations. A big part of this was the fact that I didn't know how to dress for them, or even how to speak in front of people my dad's age. I'll never forget the time a mentor pulled me aside and asked me to change before a meeting because my outfit was very much conveying "adult toddler who is going for Zooey Deschanel but ending up with Raggedy Ann." Okay, that quote is mine, and she put it much more nicely. But I wasn't dressing like the badass professional I wanted to be.

It was shortly after this that I started #NeutralLife, a hashtag-slash-lifestyle choice in which I reduced 85 percent of my wardrobe down to neutral, versatile, simply cut investment pieces. I got things like blazers and leather bags and nude heels. I wanted to, in one fell swoop, get rid of all the frilly dresses that made me feel like a kid and start feeling each day like a Real Businesswoman. I took a radical approach to overhauling my wardrobe because I had big goals for it—and big leaps to make in my own self-perception.

Part of creating the wardrobe of the woman I wanted to be was following a few key people on social media who made style—especially for the workplace—feel like something I could actually be good at and something I could manage without it dominating my morning routine. In many ways, they showed me that I could actually start to feel like the chic young businesswoman I had in my head, as long as I was smart about it. So, naturally, I called on them to share their insights for creating a killer professional wardrobe.

Ella CERON

Digital West Coast Editor, *Teen Vogue*

I don't have any one mantra for my work style, and I believe that anything I wear to work should be able to translate to "weekend wear." Having different closets is really limiting. Two things always make it easy: tons of black, and basic designer items that go with anything and everything else that's in my closet. I don't hunt for labels so much as I try to invest in quality—but consignment stores and sample sales mean you're still getting amazing pieces for way less.

Ella's Rules:

1. **Shoes will always upgrade any outfit, and the better made they are, the longer they will last you.** It's worth investing more in timeless styles you'll use every day for years. (And better-made heels are always more comfortable.)

2. **A solid haircut absolutely counts as part of your wardrobe and appearance.** (But spending more on a haircut doesn't necessarily make it better, and if you've found the perfect stylist for less, never let that stylist go.)

3. **A great jacket.** I love my leather jacket, but if you have a trench or coat you adore, that counts. It ties your look together no matter what you're wearing that day.

Amanda MULL

**Managing Editor,
PurseBlog.com**

My main work wardrobe goal is finding clothes that telegraph both professionalism and my own particular aesthetic. Comfort is also important to me, which I think is an underrated virtue in professional wardrobes; workdays can be long and busy, and having clothes in which you look and feel confident for extended periods eliminates what is potentially a big stressor.

Amanda's Rules:

1. **A bag with just the right amount of personality.** People tend to notice a bag because we carry the same one frequently, so it's important to choose a bag that looks sophisticated and reflects the persona you want to convey to your colleagues.

2. **Black ankle boots.** Booties have become something of a year-round option, so having a nice, neutral, versatile pair makes it easier to get dressed and look put together.

3. **A good bra.** It's nonintuitive, but especially for women with large chests, having a professionally fitted, high-quality bra will make the rest of your work wardrobe fit better.

The
signature
dress.

Tyler McCALL

**Deputy Editor,
Fashionista.com**

I work for a digital fashion outlet,
which means I don't really have to live
by standard "professional dressing" rules
(and thank God, because I do not look
good in blazers). My MO when it comes to
building my work wardrobe is centered around buying
high-quality accessories and basics that can make any outfit
look expensive.

Tyler's Rules:

1. **An upscale work bag.** It doesn't have to be from a luxury label, but nothing
   pulls your look together faster than a nice bag. (N.B.: Mine is a 3.1 Phillip
   Lim Pashli.)

2. **A go-to dress.** No matter what you do, everyone needs one dress they can
   throw on and instantly feel like a boss bitch. (N.B.: Mine is Kate Spade.)

3. **Signature accessories.** Your wardrobe should reflect you, so it's okay
   to have fun with it! I love flats, so I'm always down to shell out for a flashy
   or quirky pair.

Chapter 4

How to Be Your Own Italian Grandmother

Feed yourself like you were a welcome guest in your own home, not an ex you were trying to get rid of.

Most of my memories of my mother are in the kitchen. Cooking wasn't her only area of expertise, but the kitchen always felt like her domain, a place that, to me, was at once magical and deeply familiar. Nearly every night I sat on the counter or ran around her feet, tasting and stirring and, eventually, chopping, helping her to make something great for dinner. Growing up in my family, restaurants were a rare luxury, and prepackaged foods were nearly unheard of.

When I'd go to friends' houses, the first thing I'd do was raid their pantries, gorging myself on snack foods. I'd marvel at my friends' abilities to dictate the food they were served, or the fact that dinosaur chicken nuggets and fries existed outside of birthday parties. I wanted nothing more than a box of Kraft Mac & Cheese when my mother was constantly serving orecchiette with broccoli rabe. My birthday breakfast request was always Cream Cheese & Strawberry Toaster Strudel, an exotic delicacy that so many of my friends seemed to get all the time.

As a result, and from what I have noticed of my friends and colleagues, much of our generation regards home cooking as simultaneously scary and far too much of a hassle. This costs us deeply in our own connection to our food and where it comes from, but it more immediately costs us in our checking account. Being one of those millennials who eschews home cooking completely for a rotating cast of Seamless orders and bar food means living an unnecessarily expensive life. On the opposite end, we have the "foodie millennials," whose pendulum has swung so far in the other direction that every meal they cook looks like some kind of Food Network competition segment. Foodie culture may have gotten us looking at a lot of well-lit pictures of spicy tuna rolls on Instagram, but it hasn't gotten us into an affordable, and effective, everyday food routine.

Now, of course, I spend a lot of time apologizing to my mother for all the shit I gave her about my own food upbringing. More than anything, the way she raised me has taught me that cooking for oneself and one's family is an imperative of everyday life, and that going out or ordering in is, without exception, a treat. This perspective is financial more than anything, and when I was young, and my family faced serious financial insecurity, home cooking and being frugal in the kitchen were crucial to our survival. Learning to cook well and often was about pragmatism first, passion second. This was true of my mother, and her mother, and her grandmother who came from Naples with a big wooden spoon that alternated between stirring her magnificent sauces and keeping her enormous family in order.

Few choices we make in life will have as much of a sustained and profound impact on our budgets as learning how to cook and embracing it as a daily necessity. (Master your kitchen, master your wallet.) Once we get over the idea that food must always be "cool" in some way, or look perfectly Instagrammable, it immediately becomes easier to make it work as an everyday thing. We should embrace the delicious-yet-utilitarian approach of the mythic Italian Grandmother: she's always whipping something up based on what's around, what's in season, and what's about to go bad. She cooks in big quantities, freezes what keeps well, and focuses more on moderation than any particular diet. A little bit of everything, too much of nothing. Her foods are filling, well seasoned, and budget friendly. (As my mother would always say, meat should be the treat, not the focus of the meal—if for no other reason than because it's expensive.) I promise, if you embrace the Italian grandmother mind-set and make cooking an everyday thing, you will set yourself on the path to mastering your own culinary domain.

To help with that, we've created the Ten Commandments for Being Your Own Italian Grandmother:

How to Be Your Own

Italian Grandmother

1. Never waste your groceries. You buy it, you find a way to eat it.

2. Think in ingredients, not in individual meals—what can you get the most out of?

3. Always big-batch and freeze your S-foods: sauces, soups, stews.

4. Think in two portions: one for tonight, one for lunch tomorrow.

5. Keep your spice rack full and your garlic basket fuller.

6. Have at least ten recipes in your back pocket that you can make by heart in under thirty minutes.

7. Make the meat the guest star of your plate, not the main character.

8. When you buy or make good bread, get extra and freeze it.

9. Know what to make from scratch and when to save yourself the trouble.

10. For big cooking days, always have a good glass of wine to sip.

We've gathered recipes and tips from a real-live Italian grandmother (my partner's grandmother). So break out that glass of wine and put away that credit card because you're not spending a regrettable amount on take-out food tonight. We're cooking!

One of the first things you'll need to take care of when deciding you're going to be "someone who cooks" is setting up a kitchen. No matter where you live—sprawling farmhouse or cramped Manhattan studio—you're going to need the same basic tools. You might fall anywhere on the current kitchen spectrum from "I don't own utensils that aren't left over from a take-out order" to "I go to Sur La Table when I'm drunk and buy zesters to relieve my tension." Personally, I fall distinctly to the latter side of that dichotomy, and I know that my habit of buying kitchen supplies out of passion instead of necessity has only ended in serious culinary remorse. The first apartment I had to myself was so small that the shower was in the kitchen (yes, literally), and yet I still justified a trip to an upscale home goods store to buy a mint-green immersion blender. Since then, through my many kitchens, I've gotten better about planning ahead and waiting to see what I need before buying it.

You may find, as you go, that a waffle iron is something you crave (and actually wish to use) every day. Or you may want three different types of blenders and food processors for your morning smoothies. Or you may need every kind of baking tray, from "muffin" to "Bundt." All of those things are dependent on who *you* are as a home cook. But according to my mom—outside of your basic pots and pans—here are the tools any budget Julia Child is going to want in her kitchen, regardless of individual recipe preferences:

Fuller HUNT

Chelsea's Mom and Domestic Goddess

Essential Kitchen Tools

- **Butcher knife:** This is your multipurpose chopping and cutting knife. I use it for all types of food and I smash garlic cloves with the side of it.

- **Bread knife:** For cutting a lot of soft/spongy things, not just bread.

- **Wood cutting board:** Wood is naturally antibacterial, easier on knives, and can be refinished as needed. I use one side for meat and one for vegetables.

- **Large mixing bowl**

- **One each of high-quality stainless pot and pan:** Invest in quality cookware and build outward from the absolute essential pot and pan.

- **Whisk:** This is essential when making a sauce with a roux, cornstarch, or a flour slurry

- **Rolling pin:** Making your own dough is cheap and easy, and the dough is totally freezable for when you need it. Also, handy for breaking up ice cubes.

- **Grater:** Box graters with options to slice and zest handle several jobs at once.

- **Wooden spatula:** To stir and cook without scratching.

- **Rubber spatula:** To scrape bowls down and get every last drop!

- **Metal spatula:** Perfect for cooking, and serving lots of baked goods.

- **Tongs:** Preferably with heat resistant, rubber-tipped ends for grabbing.

- **Peeler**

- **Small food processor:** I've had the one my mother bought me twenty-one years ago and it's been a lifesaver for when I have a lot of *mise en place* to prepare (a.k.a. chopping lots of different things) and it makes salad dressings and vinaigrettes, shreds cheese, chops herbs, and whips cream. Heck, you can even make butter in it!

- **Measuring cups and spoons:** Ones for dry ingredients and ones for liquids.

- **Baking sheet and loaf:** To get you started on your oven.

- **Quality kitchen towels:** These serve every purpose from handling hot dishes to cleaning up messes, and they cut down on paper towel costs.

- **Thermometer:** Everything from roast chicken to homemade deep-fried doughnuts will come out right.

Fuller's Rules for Buying Kitchen Supplies

a) Get some basics that you know you'll always need, and wait to see your cooking habit before buying the more elaborate stuff.

b) It's better to start with only a few high-quality items (skillets, pots, trays, etc.) than a big set of something made of crappy materials.

c) Thrift stores and garage/moving sales can be your best friend when it comes to high-quality kitchen tools and tableware — not everything needs to be new!

Once you've got your kitchen stocked with enough basic tools to actually make and serve something, what do you make? The key here is to stop thinking in terms of individual recipes and start thinking in terms of "always being able to make something with what I have at home." If you have to go out and get every single ingredient for everything you want to cook—including basic things like seasonings and oils—you are way more likely to just say, "Whatever, I'm ordering in." Having the supplies you need to whip something up with whatever ingredients you have hanging out in the fridge and, more important, being able to make it taste good is how you get truly comfortable with home cooking.

At TFD, we have zeroed in on what we feel are the basic ingredients every home cook should have in their kitchen, the bare minimum. These are the essentials, and they will take you through many a basic recipe and a whipped-together something-or-other when you come home tipsy and are hesitating between a quick pasta dish and a $30 Seamless order, I promise.

Herbs, Seasonings, and Pastes:

- **Salt and pepper:** Yes, really. Because we all need to be reminded sometimes. And upgrade your life to kosher salt and fresh-cracked pepper, because pre-ground pepper is sad.

- **Crushed red pepper:** If you're not finding a need for crushed red pepper, you aren't cooking enough good Italian food.

- **Cinnamon:** Put it in your coffee, put it in your desserts, and put it in (yes) a lot of your savory dishes.

- **Herbes de Provence:** A solid mix of savory herbs that is great for everything from roast meats to root vegetables.

- **Good chicken bouillon:** Everyone needs to be able to make some stock on a moment's notice, so get some of the good stuff, like the bouillon paste.

- **Curry paste:** Getting in the habit of making curries means you'll always have an awesome way to use your proteins and vegetables, and something delicious to pair your rice with.
- **Chili paste/dried chilis:** Are you #TeamSpicy? You should be. And if you are, you'll need to up your chili game significantly.
- **Old Bay:** I'm from Maryland, so I am legally required to tell you that Old Bay makes almost everything more delicious, including and especially popcorn.
- **Garlic and yellow onions:** Add rich, savory, nearly calorie-free flavor to basically any dish? Yes, please.

Oils and Sauces:

- **Olive oil:** Get good olive oil, and if you don't believe it makes a difference, Google it. Bad olive oil is kind of scary.
- **Soy sauce:** Soy sauce is like salt on steroids, because it makes things salty *and* umami. Always have good soy sauce on hand.
- **Sesame oil:** Want a fragrant oil that makes things taste delicious that isn't olive oil? Sesame oil is your friend—just don't use too much, because one small spoonful is like being drop-kicked by an angry sesame seed.
- **Vinegar:** Step up your vinegar game and get a few: balsamic, red wine, white wine, rice wine.
- **Good mustard:** Yellow mustard makes angels cry, and good mustard (whether spicy Chinese mustard or whole-grain French mustard) is the base of so many delicious sauces and dressings. But more on that later.
- **Cooking wine:** I always say don't cook with anything you wouldn't drink, for two reasons: a) the flavor is better, and b) you'll usually end up drinking some of it with the meal!

Baking Basics:

- **Flour:** Creamy sauces, biscuits, fancy things you feel like baking one rainy weekend? All of them require some good flour, always to have on hand.
- **Butter:** And yes, if you use it often, you should keep it, covered, on the counter. Fridge butter is a sin.
- **Sugar:** Go crazy, get a few different kinds for different things!
- **Baking soda and powder:** You never need them until you do.

You've stocked your kitchen. Now you are ready to get cooking. From impressing friends on a dime to having a satisfying Sunday dinner that doesn't take seven hours of prep, you need to have some serious go-tos when it comes to recipes. We think that there are six truly crucial situations in which it's easy to default to the more expensive option (i.e., going out or getting delivery) but all you might need is a key recipe that you know like the back of your hand, to save you from spending unnecessarily. For us, those situations are:

The Recipes!

1. The cocktail.

2. The recipe that uses whatever you have in your fridge.

3. The meal you can make big and freeze for later.

4. The Sunday dinner that doesn't take all day.

5. The impressive-but-easy dessert.

6. The take-out alternative that keeps you off Seamless.

THE RUBIK'S SPRITZ

This is a drink Lauren and I first saw while browsing Instagram. We tracked it down to a chic Manhattan bar so we could try it for ourselves. It does require you to get a large ice cube tray, but if you're at all into home cocktail making, those big cubes are well worth it. And this drink is the ultimate "Are you a mixologist?!?!" drink to break out while entertaining that requires almost zero effort or skill.

You will need:

- 2 liqueurs of your choice (we like things like Aperol, Campari, and St-Germain)
- 1 12-ounce bottle sparkling water
- 1 750ml bottle Prosecco
- Garnish (sliced citrus, herbs, berries, etc.)

To make this drink, you simply:

- Freeze 1 part liqueur to 4 parts sparkling water in an eight-cube extra-large ice cube tray.
- Once frozen, put two cubes each into four large wineglasses or other decorative glasses of your choice.
- Pour 4 ounces of Prosecco over each pair of ice cubes and top with 1 ounce of sparkling water in each glass.
- Garnish according to your liqueurs of choice and serve.

Great liquor/herb pairings!

- Aperol & Rosemary
- Campari & Thyme
- Limoncello & Mint

BASIC
QUICHE

PREP: 20 MINS | COOK TIME: 40 MINS
MAKES: 4-6 SERVINGS

When it comes to the standby recipes that everyone should be able to make with their eyes closed, few things are more universal than a basic quiche. The thing about a quiche is, when made crustless, the process takes only a few minutes from start to finish, and you can put to use nearly any leftover protein, veg, or cheese you have lying around in your fridge. Few things are more important to becoming a master home chef than being able to make the best of what you already have around—from the freezer, the back of the cupboard, or the about-to-expire packages in your fridge. And few recipes make better use of what you have than a good crustless quiche.

For this quiche, we used leeks, sausage, and pecorino cheese, but we encourage you to fill your quiches with anything from bacon to potatoes to spinach to feta. Everything is good in a quiche.

You will need:

- Butter for greasing the baking dish
- 3 large sweet Italian sausages, de-cased and crumbled
- 3 leeks, trimmed, washed, and thinly sliced
- Olive oil (optional)
- 3 cloves garlic, minced
- Salt and pepper to taste
- 8 large eggs
- ½ cup whole milk
- 2 ounces (½ cup) grated Pecorino Romano
- 1 tablespoon French mustard

Method:

- Preheat the oven to 375°F and lightly butter a 9 x 9-inch baking dish.
- In a large skillet over medium-high heat, cook the crumbled sausage until caramelized, about 8 minutes. Remove the cooked sausage from the pan, leaving the drippings.

-Add the leeks to the drippings in the pan, adding a touch of olive oil as needed to properly coat the leeks. After 2 minutes of cooking, while stirring the leeks, add the garlic. Lightly season the mixture with salt and pepper, and cook, stirring frequently, until the leek-and-garlic mixture is softened and cooked through, about 6 minutes total.

-While cooking down the leeks and garlic, in a large bowl mix together the eggs, milk, three-quarters of the cheese, the mustard, and a pinch of salt and pepper. Set aside.

-When the leek, garlic, and sausage mixture is fully cooked, add to the egg mixture. Stir well and pour into the prepared baking dish. Top with the rest of the cheese.

-Bake the quiche for 40 minutes, or until the quiche is golden brown and firm throughout.

-Allow quiche to cool 10 minutes before slicing and serving.

Bonus!

THE ULTIMATE VINAIGRETTE

Pair your quiche with the perfect green salad, topped with **Chelsea's famous vinaigrette.** To make the dressing, simply mix together:

- 3 tablespoons vinegar
- 2 tablespoons oil
- 1½ tablespoons soy sauce
- 1½ tablespoons honey
- 1 tablespoon hot mustard (Chinese and French mustard are both great here)
- Several big cracks of black pepper

THE MEAL YOU CAN MAKE BIG AND FREEZE FOR LATER

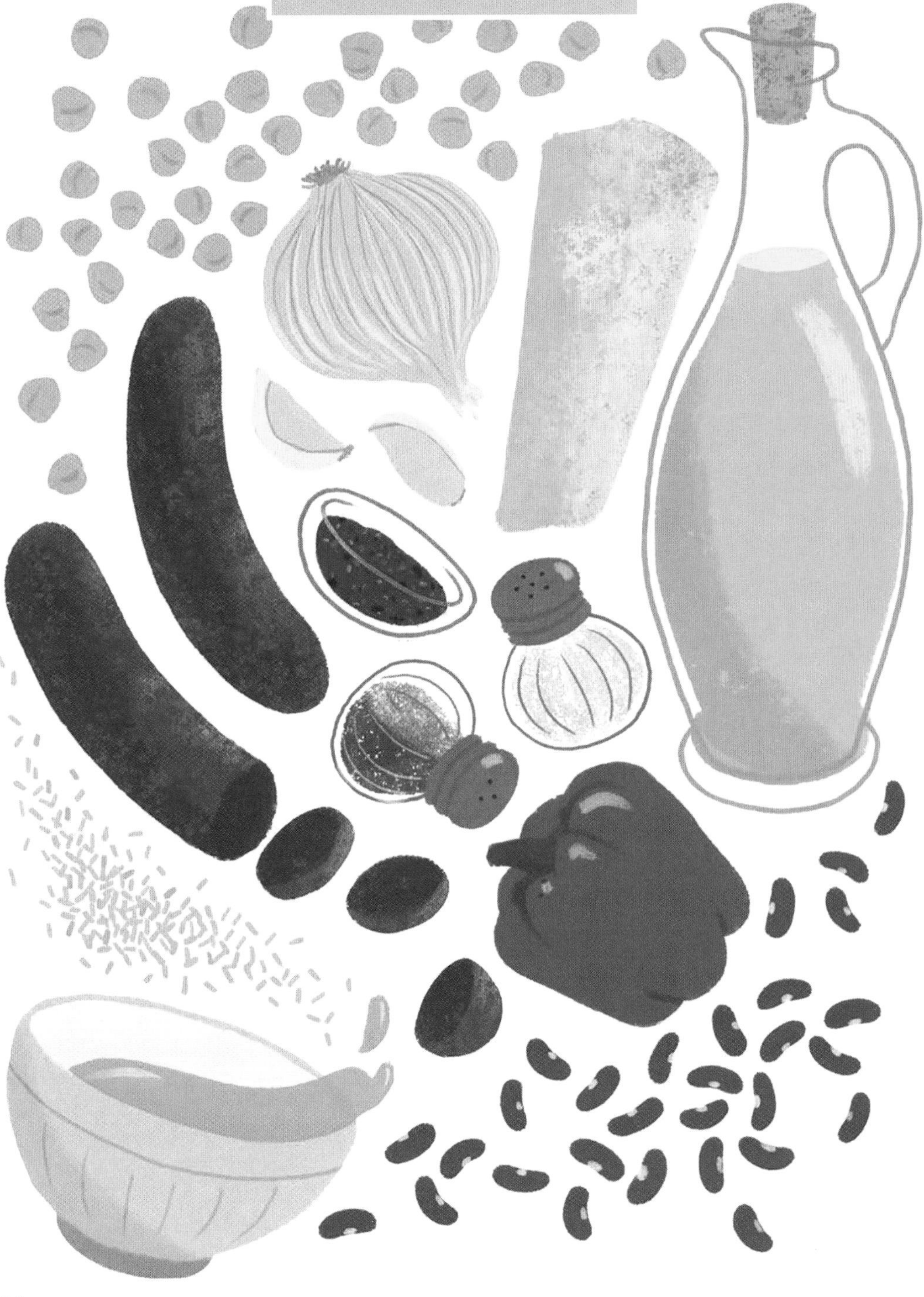

MY MOM'S SOUL-WARMING RED BEANS AND RICE

**PREP: 30 MINS | COOK TIME: 1 HOUR
MAKES: ABOUT 6 QUARTS OF SOUP, TO SERVE
2 TO 4 PEOPLE AND FREEZE THE REST**

Freezing food properly is one of the biggest "lifestyle" changes you can make to your budget—it allows you to shop more on sale, get good deals in bulk, and ensure you're less tempted to order takeout because there's always something delicious waiting to be defrosted. To get started on the "frozen food master" train, we have my slightly adapted version of a staple dish I had growing up that is perfect to make in big batches and freeze for cold winter nights: **My Mom's Soul-Warming Red Beans and Rice.**

You will need:

- 1 regular pack hot Italian sausages (about six sausages)
- 1 to 2 tablespoons olive oil
- 1 large yellow onion, chopped
- 2 large green bell peppers, chopped
- 6 large cloves garlic, chopped
- Salt and pepper to taste
- 2 15-ounce cans red kidney beans, drained
- 1 15-ounce can garbanzo beans, drained
- 1 rind of Pecorino or Parmesan
- 1 32-ounce box unsalted chicken stock
- 3 cups salted chicken broth
- 2 tablespoons chili garlic sauce
- 2 cups uncooked white rice
- Grated Pecorino or Parmesan, for garnish

Method:

–In a large skillet, sauté the crumbled sausage over medium-high heat until the fat is rendered and the sausage is nice and caramelized, about 8 minutes.

–Remove the sausage and set it aside, then add enough olive oil to the sausage drippings to coat the bottom of the pan. Reduce the heat to medium. Add the onion and bell peppers and let them soften for a few minutes, then, once they are slightly soft, after about 2 minutes, add the garlic.

–Sauté the vegetables together, adding a pinch of salt and pepper, until they are soft throughout, about 8 minutes.

–In your largest soup pot, place the sausage, kidney beans, garbanzo beans, cheese rind, and veggies. Cook together for 3 to 4 minutes.

–Add the unsalted chicken stock, salted chicken broth, and chili garlic sauce, stirring to combine. Cover and let simmer over medium-low heat for about 30 minutes.

–While the soup is simmering, prepare the rice according to package instructions, lightly salting it. Do not add the rice to the cooking soup, or it will overcook.

–Taste the soup after 30 minutes and add salt and pepper to taste.

To serve:

Put a small serving (about ½ cup) of rice in the bottom of a soup bowl and ladle several generous spoonfuls of soup over it, filling the bowl. Top with a bit of freshly grated Pecorino or Parmesan.

To store:

Take half of your prepared soup and allow it to cool to room temperature. Freeze in one or two batches, without rice. To serve, simply reheat, adding a portion of freshly-cooked rice.

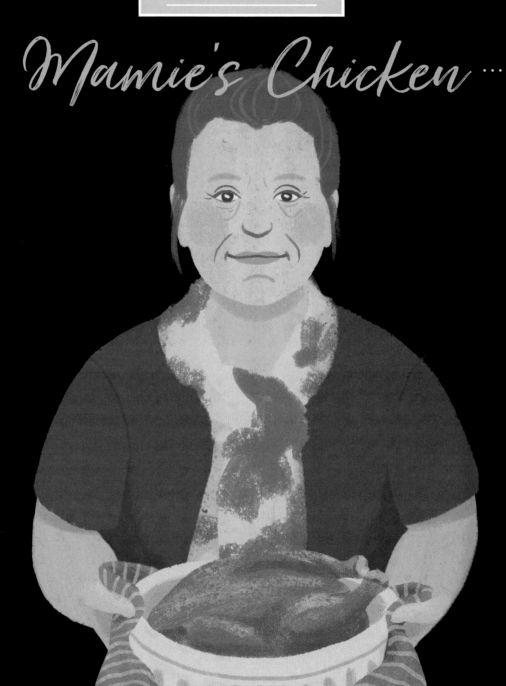

THE SUNDAY DINNER THAT
DOESN'T TAKE ALL DAY

Mamie's Chicken ...

PREP TIME: 20 MINS | COOK TIME: APPROXIMATELY 1 1/4 HOURS | MAKES: 4-6 SERVINGS

When it comes to people who have fostered my love of cooking and taught me the importance of having a solid connection to the food you eat, second only to my mother is Mamie, my partner's grandmother. A farmer of Italian roots who has spent her life in the South of France tending her animals, vineyards, and crops, every simple meal at her (offensively picturesque) farmhouse is the kind of thing you remember for years to come. Her philosophy has always been simple: good, seasonal products, using every bit of everything you can, and never trimming the fat. And while her response to "How do you make this taste so good?" is always "Oh, it's nothing, I just do it!," Lauren and I were able to follow her intently while she made her most beloved and classic recipe of all: her Roast Garlic Chicken with Fries (she served it with fresh blanched string beans, but any easy veg will do!). It's a simple recipe, and it's a manageable and lovely way to spend a Sunday with a few loved ones. And you can buy yourself the cheapest-ever ticket to the South of France by making this meal at home.

You will need:

- 1 medium-size, high-quality whole chicken with bag of organ goodies
- 10 cloves garlic
- Salt and pepper
- Several large pieces of stale, dry baguette, coarsely chopped
- 2 tablespoons cooking oil, such as vegetable or canola oil, not olive oil
- String to truss the chicken
- 1 tablespoon butter or animal fat, such as duck fat
- ½ cup low-sodium chicken stock or broth

Method:

- Preheat the oven to 375°F and place the chicken in a large ceramic baking dish.
- To make the filling, crush and peel the cloves of garlic and mash them together with the liver and kidneys from the chicken, liberally adding salt and pepper. Mix the garlic mixture with the bread pieces and 1 tablespoon cooking oil. Stuff the entire mixture into the chicken's opening and truss (this basically means tying the chicken up tight with a kitchen needle and thread—there are plenty of great tutorials available online!).
- Rub the outside of the chicken with a mixture of the butter and the remaining 1 tablespoon oil, and liberally salt and pepper the entire outside of the chicken. Make sure to get the bottom.
- Cook the chicken according to its size until cooked through and golden brown, making sure to baste it in its own juices at least three times (I test for doneness by cutting a little slice between the body and the thigh of the chicken, and making sure the juices run clear, but you can also use a meat thermometer and look for an internal temperature of about 170°F). Remove the chicken and allow it to rest for at least 5 minutes before carving.
- Carve the chicken into quadrants in the ceramic dish, allowing its juices to collect in the dish. Transfer the quadrants to a cutting board and fully carve. In the ceramic dish, add the stock to deglaze and get all of the lovely chicken bits. Pour all of the liquid into a nice serving bowl—this is your jus, and it should be liberally doused over everything and sopped up with good bread. (The garlicky bready chunks from the inside of the chicken should also be put in their own little bowl and passed around with the jus.)

Mamie's FAMOUS FRIES

**PREP: 30 MINS | COOK TIME: 10-12 MINS
PER BATCH | MAKES: 4-6 SERVINGS**

You will need:

- 10 medium yellow potatoes, peeled and placed in a large bowl of room-temperature water to cover
- 1 32-ounce bottle of canola or sunflower oil
- Salt
- 1 approximately 8-ounce container of duck fat or other animal fat

Method: (To see a video of the fry technique, go to TheFinancialDiet.com/BookResources)

–The key to these Famous Fries—and they really are in their own category of food, frankly—is how they are cut. Mamie's technique is simple: Cut the potato in half lengthwise. Holding one of the halves in your hand with the flat side facing toward you, begin to cut a half-inch wedge, slicing at a shallow angle from the outside toward the center. But don't slice all the way through—stop the knife about halfway to the center and crack off the wedge, leaving a rough surface that will puff up when fried—like delicious, crispy little fry pillows in the oil.

–Start the fry prep about halfway into your chicken's cook time.

–Once your potatoes are peeled and in a large bowl of cool water, cut each of them according to Mamie's technique. As the fries are cut, place them back in the water bowl and continue to let them soak. When all of your fries are prepped, in a Dutch oven or other fry-ready apparatus, bring the oil to 375°F and start by testing a few fries, making sure to pat dry every potato batch before you fry it! They should float to the top and start bubbling immediately. Once the oil is ready, fry up the potatoes in four or five batches for 10 to 12 minutes each or until golden brown and crispy. Transfer them immediately to a paper towel–lined dish, salt liberally, and serve while piping hot. Make sure to try some jus on your fries, too.

KEY LIME PIE

**PREP: 10 MINS | COOK TIME: 20 MINS
PLUS TIME TO COOL | MAKES: 6-8 SERVINGS**

Everyone needs to have a dessert that they get to feel amazing about, one that requires zero effort and few ingredients but gives you the joy of being able to serve a homemade dessert at the end of a good meal. These are two favorites of ours, and both requirew very few ingredients. We promise that anyone can make these perfectly on the first try.

You will need:

- 4 large egg yolks
- 1 12-to-14-ounce can sweetened condensed milk
- ½ cup lime juice (you'll need about 5 small to medium limes)
- 1 ½ teaspoons lime zest for the filling (optional), plus 1 ½ teaspoons lime zest for the garnish
- 1 graham cracker crust (or make your own)
- 1 cup heavy cream
- 2 tablespoons confectioners' sugar (granulated sugar will do in a pinch)
- 1 teaspoon vanilla extract

Method:

- Preheat the oven to 325°F.
- To make the filling, mix together the egg yolks, sweetened condensed milk, and lime juice—just three ingredients! You can also add 1½ teaspoons lime zest if you like, to make it extra-limey.
- Pour the filling into the piecrust and bake for 20 minutes, or until the pie is wobbly but firm throughout and the edges are very lightly golden brown.
- While the pie is baking, whip together the cream, sugar, and vanilla until the whipped cream has formed stiff peaks.
- Once the pie has cooled completely, cover it with a thick layer of whipped cream and sprinkle with 1½ teaspoons lime zest. Enjoy!

CHOCOLATE MOUSSE

PREP: 10 MINS | COOK TIME: 15 MINS PLUS SEVERAL HOURS' COOLING TIME MAKES: 6 SERVINGS

You will need:

- 2 cups heavy cream
- 8 ounces chocolate (you can do dark or milk, or a mixture of both, depending on how sweet you prefer your mousse to be)
- 1 teaspoon vanilla extract
- Optional: orange zest, mint extract, raspberry puree, cayenne.

Method:

- Heat the cream in a medium saucepan over medium heat until it has started to gently bubble.
- Whisk in the chocolate with a wire whisk until it is fully melted, then add the vanilla. (If the mixture isn't sweet enough for your taste, you can add a bit of confectioners' sugar here.)
- If you want to add any additional flavorings to the chocolate, such as orange or mint, add them here.
- Pour the mixture into a heat-safe container and allow to cool to room temperature, then cool in the refrigerator until fully chilled.
- Whip the chocolate cream in a chilled bowl until it's at a thickness slightly thicker than whipped cream.
- Let the whipped chocolate sit for at least 15 minutes before serving.
- Serve in small bowls or cups, garnished to your taste!

10-MINUTE THAI BASIL CHICKEN

a culinary genealogy
THE WOKS OF LIFE

The Woks of Life is one of Lauren and my favorite cooking blogs—their recipes are delicious and accessible and make you feel like you are part of the family that maintains and updates it together from all over the world. Here is one of their favorite recipes for beginners looking to satisfy that take-out craving.

You will need:

- 3 to 4 tablespoons oil
- 3 Thai or Holland chilies, de-seeded (if desired)
- 3 shallots, thinly sliced
- 5 cloves garlic, sliced
- 1 pound ground chicken
- 2 teaspoons sugar or honey
- 2 tablespoons soy sauce
- 1 tablespoon fish sauce
- 1/3 cup low-sodium chicken broth or water
- 1 bunch holy or Thai basil leaves

Method:

– In a wok over high heat, place the oil, chilies, shallots, and garlic and stir fry for 1 to 2 minutes. Add the ground chicken and stir fry for 2 minutes, breaking up the chicken into small bits.

– Add the sugar, soy sauce, and fish sauce. Stir fry for 1 minute more, then deglaze the pan with the broth. Because your pan is over high heat, the liquid should cook off very quickly. Add the basil, and stir fry until wilted. Serve over rice.

Here's the minute-by-minute breakdown to truly make it a 10-minute meal:

Minute 1: Walk leisurely over to your fridge and pull out a package of ground chicken. Then you're going to chop up 3 chilies. They don't have to be pretty.

Minute 2: Peel and slice 3 shallots. A good trick: cutting off both ends, sweeping your knife lengthwise across the shallot, and peeling off the outside in one fell swoop before slicing. Oh, and if you can't find shallots, a red onion will do just fine.

Minute 3: Following the same pattern from the previous step, you're going to slice 5 cloves of garlic. Hint: smashing them with the side of your knife makes 'em a lot easier to peel. Yeah garlic!

Minute 4: Heat a wok over high heat (not medium high. HIGH.), and then add a few tablespoons of oil, along with your prepared chilies, shallots, and garlic.

Minute 5: Allow said oil, chilies, shallots, and garlic to do their work in said wok, stirring occasionally to help them along a bit.

Minute 6: Add the ground chicken and start breaking it up.

Minute 7: Continue cooking the ground chicken until browned. How is this happening so quickly? Answer: your stove is cranked up as high as it will go.

Minute 8: Throw in some sugar, soy sauce, and fish sauce, and stir fry everything together. You are a kitchen genius.

Minute 9: Deglaze the pan with broth and toss in a bunch of Thai basil leaves.

Minute 10: You're almost home free. Just continue stir-frying over high heat until most of the liquid is cooked off and the basil is wilted.

Serve with your favorite rice!

Little Rules for Mastering the

Grocery store

Bring two shopping bags, one you fill exclusively with produce, the other with everything else *(this keeps your groceries healthy, less meat-based, less processed, and therefore less expensive).*

Stock up on the cheap, filling, long-lasting stuff, like:
- Dry grains,
- Canned beans
- Frozen vegetables
- Bouillon

Get to know your grocer's butcher, and start getting more creative with the cuts of meats you work with. *(Chicken thighs are much cheaper, more delicious, and versatile than chicken breast, for example.)*

Never go shopping while hungry, tipsy, or upset.

Automate online purchases and buy in bulk for things like toiletries and cleaning supplies: it's almost always more cost-effective than at the grocery store.

$$$

Learn to buy on sale and freeze where possible.

1/2 OFF!

Never go shopping without a list (that plans out at least a week's worth of meals).

Mastering a few basic recipes and stocking your kitchen with the things you most need (both in terms of tools and ingredients) means, more than anything, always being prepared—the essence of being a home cook. Making everything into a four-star production that requires its own trip to the grocery store and the painstaking searching of a dozen food blogs means you are less inclined to cook and you don't consider it a natural part of being an adult human. You should aspire to "throw something together" that actually tastes great and doesn't make you feel like a wet bag of sodium. Being an Italian grandmother isn't about how many crazy, complicated, social media–ready recipes you can master—it's about being comfortable in your kitchen and spending much less to get much more out of it.

Chapter 5

How to Feel Good in the Place You Live

Create the kind of home a grown-up lives in.

You should have seen my first apartment. Well, actually, if we're being technical about this—and I hope we are; this is a book about money, after all!—it was a room in a house. I lived with three bros in a big, two-story place in suburban Maryland, complete with pool and near-restaurant-size wet bar and what often passed for a dance floor. This house setup, both gender-wise and layout-wise, meant two things: there was always a party, and my room had to be my girly sanctuary. I had zero say over the rest of the house's layout (both because it was owned by two of my bro roommates and because I had no money to contribute to furniture or decor even if I had wanted to), and I also had zero say over where and when the parties would happen. I once came home to an entire dead pig in my bathtub, in preparation for a roast I was unaware was on the calendar. The house was a place of mostly fantastic chaos, constantly running video game tournaments, and the pouring of shots and playing of floating beer pong in the massive swimming pool.

This also meant that my tiny bedroom, big enough for only a twin bed and a meager desk, was the only place in which I could both express myself aesthetically and relax. Relaxing, I thought, called for blue, and since I was an idiotic twenty-year-old with no taste, the blue expressed itself in the form of Tiffany-box blue, a truly unforgivable wall color. I wish someone had told me that wall-to-wall in an aggressive blue would in fact make it feel much smaller and more claustrophobic, but I wouldn't have listened to them anyway. I wanted what I wanted, and that meant a bright blue room with baroque black-and-white curtains (don't ask), a ridiculously elaborate work chair whose seat was six inches too short for my desk, and a smattering of whatever IKEA accessories I could afford at the time.

My interior design Rumspringa overwhelmed any practicality in what I was actually buying and, looking back, I of course feel a little cringe-y about how proud I was of such an objectively ridiculous living space. But I also feel deeply nostalgic, as we all often do for our first homes away from home. The room was janky and oppressive at the same time, and the curtains looked like something out of a Victorian brothel as imagined by Epcot, but it was mine. I loved it and, more important, felt so deeply grateful for everything I had there.

Creating a home that makes you feel wonderful is (in my humble opinion) a gift you give yourself that echoes through the rest of your life (and yes, you can put that on a greeting card). A bedroom you love is one in which you want to have an organized, well-cared-for wardrobe, which means less money spent replacing your battered items. A happy, practical, smartly appointed kitchen is one you actually *want* to cook in, which means much less money spent eating out or ordering in. A chic and comfortable living room means more entertaining at home and embracing the lost art of dinner parties (always cheaper than doing drinks and a restaurant dinner!). Even a Zen, candle-filled, clean bathroom is one in which you want to spend time doing home spa treatments instead of feeling like you have to go somewhere expensive to feel beautiful.

If you create the home that is most attuned to your life and somewhere you really enjoy being, everything benefits. And learning to be grateful for the space you have created will mean you spend less money trying to keep up with your own unrealistic expectations for how your home *should* look. It's important to remind ourselves to be grateful and to think as proactively as possible about our home. I'd like to own property someday, so sacrificing on rent now and not paying for things I can't afford is a fair exchange. Being smart about when and where I invest in furniture or decor, and accepting that I can't have everything nice all at once, is just part of the mentality I have to adopt, but that doesn't mean I can't enjoy where I am at the present moment.

For most of us, the space we live in dictates the biggest chunk of our budget and is, in many cases, an investment, so it's crucial we treat our home decisions with as much thought and care as any other spending choice. If you are someone who knows you want to own your own home—and it's often an excellent move money-wise, though the individual costs and benefits vary depending on where you live, of course—you have to start planning for that decision long before you execute on it. You have to save, and rent below your means, so that you can have the down payment when it comes time to make it, even if that means not getting everything you want in your rentals.

But before we get into the details of buying (if and when the time is right for you), you need to master renting, as very few of us go straight from our parents' place to our own piece of property. This may sound aggressive, but essentially it's important to remember that as a renter, it's always your job to protect yourself, first and foremost. This means looking for a fairly priced unit in your city and not getting screwed over, especially if you are new in town (find locals on the Internet to talk to, and do tons of research on your own!). If you have a broker, make sure you negotiate their fee, and don't feel shy about asking to see many (many!) different places until you find the one that's right for you.

When you move in, take lots of photos to document the state of the place, and do the same when you leave. If you're living with roommates, your name better be on that lease (if there is no legal record of you living somewhere, you have zero recourse if anything shady happens—from the roommates or from the landlord). When you correspond with your management or landlord, always do it in writing so you have a record of the conversation—and make sure every rent check comes with a record, too. It's your job to be a respectful and responsible tenant, but it's also your landlord's job to maintain the place and give you what you're owed (like functioning utilities, and your security deposit back). The only way to make sure you have that stuff covered is by being proactive and careful, and documenting what happens. It sounds like a lot, but as a renter, you are often at the whim of everyone else (the landlord, the supers, the owner of the building), and protecting yourself up front means a lot fewer headaches in the future.

Should I Rent It?

(Because the right place for you is not just about how cute it is,
it's about the numbers and the priorities that actually matter in the long term.)

☐ Is the rent 30 percent of my monthly income or less?

☐ Is there a broker's fee?

☐ If so, can you try and negotiate it down?

☐ Are utilities included?

☐ Are pets allowed? Is there a fee?

☐ Can I pay rent online?

☐ Is rent stabilized or controlled?

☐ Who do I call with a maintenance problem?

☐ Do I need a guarantor?

☐ Do I need a cosigner?

☐ Can I break the lease if need be? What are the penalties?

☐ Have I researched what I need to look out for during the walk-through? For example: *Water? Electricity? Internet connection? Cell service? Window and door up to code? Any existing damage noted and signed off on?*

Visit
TheFinancialDiet.com/BookResources to Download

"The day I started treating my home like a place I actually cared about was the day I started feeling really confident in myself. It was a proud extension of myself, instead of my awkward nest of shame."

Now that you have your home, you need to care for it. Realistically, how we appoint and maintain our living space dictates a lot of our budget. Having the confidence and knowledge of basic handiwork and design allows you to do everything from adapting furniture to fitting a color scheme to making basic repairs on a home without having to call your super five times a week. And that makes your life better and more affordable.

The first step on the road to being your own handywoman is owning and mastering the basic tools of home maintenance. No matter where you are in the home-having process, you will always need to have certain tools at your disposal and be aware of the purpose they serve (and, most important, how not to kill yourself or someone else while using them). To find out the ultimate starter tool kit, I spoke to my mom, who's been house-flipping since before I could walk.

Fuller HUNT

Chelsea's Mom and Domestic Goddess

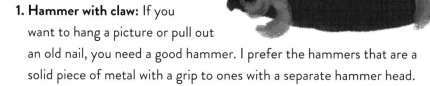

Chelsea's Mom's Tool Kit Every Woman Needs in Her Home

1. **Hammer with claw:** If you want to hang a picture or pull out an old nail, you need a good hammer. I prefer the hammers that are a solid piece of metal with a grip to ones with a separate hammer head.

2. **11-in-1 screwdriver:** There are a lot of jobs around the house, including assembling flat-pack furniture, that a power drill is too much for. No matter the job, the work is always easier with the right tool, so it's good to have options.

3. **Handheld saw and miter box:** There is no way to cut a straight edge or a miter (a joint made between two pieces of wood, a.k.a. a corner) without these tools, and you can use the saw for many other jobs.

4. **Level, a.k.a. spirit level or bubble level:** It is nigh impossible to be sure things are level without one of these. For everyday use, I find a 10-inch level does the trick, but you can download a level app that will do in a pinch.

5. **Slip-joint pliers:** For when you need to hold something still or tight or wrench open something that's stuck.

6. **Needle-nose pliers:** You can use these for everything that the slip-joint pliers are too big for, and along with the slip-joint pliers when two opposing forces are needed; i.e., open something that's stuck.

7. **Tape measure:** Enough said.

8. **Cordless drill:** This tool is a lifesaver for those jobs that are repetitive and/or require a lot of torque. It can become a power sander, a hole driller, and a buffer with the appropriate attachment. Get the lightest weight possible (without sacrificing quality) — there are lots of "best cordless drill" articles and you will have a very hard time adding your force to a drill you can barely hold up.

9. **Various screws, picture hangers, and nails:** I find that the most versatile and most used are 1½" to 2" coarse thread drywall screws and 4–5d (penny weight) finish nails.

10. **Scissors:** Duh.

11. **Masking tape and painter's tape:** These two are very versatile tools. Use the painter's tape when you're afraid to ruin a surface and masking tape when you need some serious sticking power.

Basic Home Things You Should Know How to Do:

- Change a lightbulb
- Fix a toilet lever
- Use a power drill
- Unclog a drain
- Replace a light switch
- Tighten a leaky pipe or faucet
- Find a stud
- Fix a drywall hole
- Assemble IKEA furniture

(YouTube is your friend!)

Being able to do your own basic repairs will save you a lot of money in the long and short term, and being able to rehab and improve the things you put *into* your home can be equally beneficial. Just like you should become a master of the thrift shop for upscale wardrobe items, you should be one of those people who's able to go to a junk sale, get a shoddy-looking but solid dresser, and transform it into something beautiful. We can all have the beauty and design we crave, as well as the home spaces that make us want to be productive and organized, without having to spend most of our take-home pay on a West Elm catalog.

My approach at creating a grown-up apartment is twofold:

1. You can't take things as they come.

Any budget domestic goddess *must* master some basic tools and handiwork, because it means the difference between "having to pay a lot of money if you want something to look nice and fancy" and "being able to *make* something nice and fancy, even if you got it at IKEA or World Market or a yard sale." If you can sand, paint, use drills and hammers, join together a few basic pieces of wood, attach metal legs to things, and so on, you basically have all the know-how you need to create a fully designed and decorated space.

I've revamped more furniture than I can count in my place, whitewashed and added gold accents and things like contact paper to turn my rental kitchen cabinets from "aggressively ugly mayonnaise linoleum" into what convincingly passes for "espresso wood if you don't look at it too closely for too long," which is more than good enough for me. I know that I won't have the perfect place overnight, but because I've gotten in the habit of picking furniture for its shape, size, price, and function, and accepting that anything from color to fixtures can be changed, a world of decor has opened up to me. When Lauren and I were creating the TFD office coffee station, for example, we happened to find a little wood kitchen cart while walking home from a bar. After a cleaning, a vigorous sanding, and a whitewashing, we had a chic, bright little cart to make our morning coffee on. Combined with a few other practical pieces, our office suddenly has a mini-kitchen—where it only used to have a wall.

2. You have to be honest about what you actually need.

Perhaps the biggest challenge, once you've mastered the strategy of transforming what you have and can find for cheap, is "not getting ahead of yourself." Don't fall into the trap of buying things that you want but don't actually need simply because they look nice and contribute to the image you have of what your apartment *should* look like in your head. For me, the most dangerous place is the kitchen because home cooking is my biggest hobby, and I could justify nearly every purchase with a shortsighted, "This is what I do for me. I deserve this."

I've gotten better at deciding what I will actually use and, more important, waiting to live in my apartment for a while to identify needs as they arise. That means that I might live a year in a new place before I can safely say, "Hey, we should get a high-top table for next to the door." And if I take another six months to find (and DIY into extreme cuteness) said high-top table, that's just how it works for me. The desire to fill your life with all the things that you believe will make you a more whole or realized person has to go because it drains your checking account and fills your life with clutter. And as evidenced by my twice-yearly purges, there is no shortage of useless trinkets in my life. Chances are, no matter how much you think you're streamlining your purchases, it's more than likely that you need to get rid of more things than to you need to acquire.

Once you have mastered these two modes of thinking about how to outfit your new (or refurbished) space, it's time to create (wait for it . . .) a budget! (You need a budget for your living situation most urgently if you have just moved, but even a space you're living in already should be given its own place in your spending planning.) Each room, ideally, should have its own budget (this is in addition to the actual costs of moving in, which, even if you're renting, can run you thousands of dollars in places like New York City). It's easy to see the finished product on some design blog or magazine and feel like you'll never be able to reasonably re-create what you're seeing without a professional designer and a limitless income, but almost anything is possible if you budget for it properly and are patient with the process.

To learn the art of mastering budget design, I spoke to Carrie Waller of Dream Green DIY, a designer, blogger, and all-around DIY genius, who was kind enough to share her rules for home decor.

Carrie WALLER

Creator of *Dream Green DIY*, designer, blogger, and all-around DIY genius

Ten Rules for Being a Budget Decor Master

1. Take your time: Rushing your design decisions will, more often than not, lead to choices you'll regret later on. There's nothing worse than making spontaneous investments only to change your mind in a year or two, so take your time thinking through your drapery, furniture, bedding, and lighting choices.

2. Shop secondhand: There's something oh so satisfying about finding the perfect piece among dusty castoffs at your local thrift store! It might take several trips to a particular antiques store to find just the right one-of-a-kind accent or piece of furniture, but when you do, it will probably cost a fraction of what it would at retail. And don't forget to haggle! My introductory question to a thrift store shopkeeper? "I saw that the piece was listed for $____ . Now, is that your *best* price?" A big smile goes a long way in getting a great deal, too!

3. Stick to a strict color palette: Choosing a scheme of two or three colors will help streamline your home decor purchases so that the collection of accents and furnishings is almost guaranteed to go together. It's much harder to experience buyer's remorse when your individual items all pair so well together, and a somewhat strict color palette goes a long way in achieving cohesion the *first* time.

4. **Become a coupon pro:** When it comes to making "Big Box" purchases from your favorite chain retail brands, coupons are your very best friend. Ask yourself, do you absolutely *need* to have that lamp this month? Chances are good that if you wait until next month, you could get the same lamp for 50 to 75 percent off! So, download those apps, sign up for store e-mails, and hoard those coupons and sale notices to make sure you get the very best bang for your buck.

5. **Enlist the help of a friend:** Looking to freshen up your bedroom or office with a new coat of paint? Don't call a professional painter. Instead, text your best friend! The two of you can have the room repainted in no time, and for just the cost of a can of paint. Other household projects that could be knocked out for next to nothing with a friend: landscape sprucing, doorknob replacement, furniture refinishing, drapery installation, and so much more. Who needs a contractor when you have a BFF?!

6. **Search for budget versions of designer inspiration:** It can be tempting when flipping through designer catalogs to splurge, but resist the impulse to throw your entire room budget away on a top-dollar couch, table lamp, or throw pillow. Instead, rip the pages of the catalog out and keep them tucked away in your bag as you troll local vintage shops and discount stores. You'll likely find a similar piece for a fraction of the cost, and practically no one else will have the same item.

7. **Trade within your circle:** You've heard the old adage that one man's trash is another man's treasure, and the same goes for home decor among your circle of pals. Send out a group e-mail to your closest friends asking them to gather their no longer used or loved household decorative items, and host everyone at your house for a friendly trade over pizza and a bottle of wine. Just ask everyone to place their goodies on an emptied dining-room table, and then each person can call dibs on the items that catch their eye. It doesn't cost a thing, and you could easily outfit an entire dresser, tabletop, or coffee table with decor.

8. **Shop your house:** Rather than grabbing your wallet and heading to the store for a new set of curtains or a tray for the coffee table, take five minutes to first walk from room to room in your house. You might just find what you're looking for in your own home, and a bit of clever rearranging can mask the switch up without having to lose a single penny in the process.

9. **Make your own wall art:** Things like abstract paintings, black-and-white photography, and framed collages all sport hefty price tags from big retailers. Instead of investing in mass-produced or pricey art, grab a blank canvas from the craft store (with a coupon, of course!) and splatter some acrylic paint on it! You'll be able to customize the piece to your specific aesthetic and color scheme; plus you're guaranteed to be the only person on the planet with that particular piece of art.

10. **Buy only what you love:** It should go without saying, but sometimes when we're faced with a trendy pillow, brass figurine, or piece of art at the store, we lose all sense of our budgets and *actual* needs back at home. Consider sleeping on the decision before making the final purchase and ask yourself if you really love it, or if you're just trying to keep up with the Joneses. Buying only what you truly love will make your house feel like home.

"Buying only what you truly love will make your house feel like home."

An example
of Carrie's
work in action!

Now that you have the basics of home handiwork and designing the perfect space for you on a budget, it's time to move to the (potentially) scariest part of this chapter: home owning. We cannot universally recommend that you *should* own a home, because we don't know your life or your situation or your desire. And it's not our job to tell you what will absolutely be the right "big financial decision" for you. But we *can* say that home ownership is a valuable financial decision for many people. It's both a day-to-day living space and an investment—and few investments are so immediately useful. But home ownership is sadly an art that seems to have fallen a bit by the wayside with millennials.

- **Home ownership is down 20% among millennials compared to the previous generation.**

- **Home ownership among millennials reached an all-time low in 2016.**

- **Urban areas, where millennials prefer to live, are now more expensive in terms of home values than once-coveted suburbs.**

Despite the generally bleak statistics about our generation and its debt and underemployment, we are not some lost cause, destined to float around in temp gigs and shitty apartments until some distant family member gets hit by a truck and leaves us a life-changing inheritance. I believe, if you want to be a home owner, and decide that you *will* be one, and start planning your budget and work decisions around that now, it's very possible. If you want to take on a side gig specifically to put toward a down payment, do it. If you want to reduce what you're paying in rent each month to save up more quickly, do it. If you want to move to a city where there are a lot of real estate opportunities in up-and-coming neighborhoods, do it. The point is that you can't treat buying a home, like so many financial decisions, as some vague thing that Future You will do at some undetermined point. You have to treat it as an active goal you are working toward, *not* an unrealistic pipe dream.

Three Quick Ways To Build Your Credit

1. Automate your bill payments to go through your credit card, and then your credit card to be paid off in full each month. You will get automatic good credit usage and rack up free points on the bills you were paying anyway!

2. Go through your credit report with a fine-tooth comb and pay any outstanding debts or collections—even $20 owed on an old store card counts!

3. Make the difference between the credit you *can* use and the credit you *do* use even wider: this might mean opening a new card or raising the limits on your current one while keeping your spending down.

Can I Buy It?

- How much house can I afford?
  - *Use mortgage affordability calculators to determine how much house you should be buying.*

- How much can I afford in my down payment?
  A very simplistic example and calculation of a $250,000 home:
  - 3.5 percent FHA loan (a special government loan that especially helps first-time buyers!) would be: **$8,750**
  - 5 percent down payment would be: **$12,500**
  - 20 percent down payment: **$50,000**

NOTE:
Depending on the mortgage program for which you're applying, there's going to be a specified minimum down payment amount.

- What's my credit score?

- What's my annual income?

- How much do I pay each month on debts?

- What's the term of my mortgage? How much is the mortgage rate?

- How much are the property taxes?

- How much is homeowner's insurance?

- Do I have enough money left over *after* buying?

Keep
In Mind:

−You should have anywhere from three to six months' worth of extra money saved up to pay bills in case of an emergency Also, an expert says that the average home-owner spends **2.5 to 3 percent** of a home's value each year on upkeep and maintenance. So portion out extra money per month to cover the unexpected costs of repair.

−Think about other costs associated with moving: **Packing and shipping, home inspection, title services and lender's title insurance, credit score fee, loan application fee, buying stuff to furnish the new space, and so on.**

−A good credit score is key to a good mortgage. Credit scores affect whether you qualify for a home loan, and the higher your credit score, the better the interest rate you can get. A score of **740 or higher** qualifies you for the best rates from most lenders.

740

Poor   Excellent

Navigating the world of home buying, even if you have a lot of money to work with, is not easy. And making sure you make the best decisions for you requires you to have, much like with investment, a financial Sherpa. To learn more about when to know if you're financially ready to buy a home, I spoke to friend of TFD Erica Sinchak, vice president at The Federal Savings Bank, who is certified to assist home buyers in all fifty states. We asked her how to know when your finances are ready to take the plunge.

"The scariest thing about buying a home, in a lot of ways, is that it requires you to do a not-insignificant amount of math."

Erica SINCHAK

Vice President at *The Federal Savings Bank*, and certified to assist home buyers in all fifty states

Q. How do you know if you're financially ready to buy?

There is no "right time" to buy, but there are financial risks that you are or are not comfortable taking. Your current financial position has a bearing on your ability to buy today, but ultimately, how much money you put down, where you buy, what you buy (home, condo, town house, etc.) are all decisions that depend on what your financial state needs to be in the future to sustain that purchase, and whether that is feasible.

Buying the home is actually the easy part; you can do it with 3.5 percent down (only 3.5 percent of the actual cost of the house)! The unknown future expenses, lifestyle, and economic changes should factor into your decision-making process. The risks you face in purchasing a home are well documented after the housing crisis and should be considered—spending below your means applies just as much to home buying as it does to, say, using credit cards. Additionally, many expenses exist that are tied to each individual's unique capabilities as a home owner.

The questions you should ask yourself when considering buying a home are:

• **How long could you make payments without your job?**
• **What happens if your property taxes increase?**
• **How soon do you want to sell your home?**
• **Are you comfortable taking a loss to sell, if necessary?**
• **Are you prepared to cover unknown large expenses in the future (roof,**

furnace, air-conditioning)?

• **Will you have to pay service providers to perform common tasks?**

There are many variables and financial risks in the way people live and their corresponding housing market across America. Research your area and become knowledgeable about all the variables. Monetize these variables and make educated decisions as to when you are truly "ready to buy" and what your financial situation should look like now and into the future.

The following are general financial principles that all home buyers should consider:

- **Income Stability**—It's generally advisable to have been at the same job, or at least in the same industry, for at least two years. Would it hypothetically be easy for you to find another job?
- **Savings**—The minimum required down payment for a home is 3.5 percent, but the more you can give up front, the more favorable your mortgage terms. You should also have savings that will cover unforeseeable expenses. Prove your ability and discipline to save money.
- **Credit**—Strive for a credit score in the "good" range (700+) and you will gain access to the best mortgage rates. If you're stretched so thin that you are forced to make purchases on your credit card (and can't pay it off at the end of the month), you might reconsider buying a home until expenses are controlled.

Bonus: in many areas across the country, your mortgage will cost less than rent!

Q. What are some things someone should look for in a mortgage?

Deciding where to shop for a mortgage and whose advice to trust can be intimidating! My best advice is to shop around with a few different lenders (local and national banks, and credit unions if you belong to one). Find someone you trust with low, fixed rates and reasonable fees. Don't be tricked by low introductory/adjustable rates or rates that are well below the competition. The phrase "too good to be true" is important in a business as complex as mortgages.

Finding the place you love, renting or buying it in the savviest way possible, and living in it with know-how and care for the things you own is one of the biggest steps to getting control over your budget and your future. Living costs are the biggest portion of our budgets, usually, and represent so much about how we prioritize our money. It's not scary (or hard!) to get good at this stuff; it's liberating. We shouldn't be oversized kids playing house in the places we live. We should be the kind of grown-ups who have tool kits and five-year plans, who aren't completely thrown off by every minor problem. Having control over how we live feels good—trust me.

Chapter 6

How to Be a Miranda, Not a Carrie

There's nothing more cringeworthy than having a relationship be your financial plan.

It's a safe (if not too conservative) estimate to say that since the age of sixteen, I have watched each episode of *Sex and the City* about fifteen times. I came into womanhood, in many ways, guided by Carrie, Samantha, Miranda, and Charlotte, relying on them to answer the questions I was much too shy to ask, and I learned lessons from their mistakes. I coveted the outfits and dreamed of what life must be like in New York City for a group of single, self-assured, carefree women. As it happened, I made my own move to the Big Apple when I was a cool decade younger than the *SATC* gals, firmly in a long-term relationship, and certainly without a core group of female peers whose disposable income and relationship status lent themselves to endless nights sipping martinis and cruising the latest clubs. In short, my life in New York has been largely average, and I've learned—as anyone learns after they spend more than a week here—that the world of Carrie Bradshaw is only available to literal millionaires, and the fact that they passed her life off as doable on a second-tier newspaper columnist's wages is nothing short of criminal.

As a writer living in the city, I can confirm that not even the most handsomely compensated editor of some venture capitalist–backed media start-up could live Carrie's life, let alone the person writing the 1998 equivalent of listicles about dicks. The *Sex and the City* world was pure fantasy, no more attainable to the average woman than a Jane Austen novel. But that didn't matter, and shouldn't: no matter what anyone says (and I firmly believe anyone who says this sort of thing hasn't really watched the show), *Sex and the City* was fucking awesome. It was awesome beyond anything we have seen on TV since, in my opinion—to see those four women flirting openly with the big 4-0, refusing to settle or to depend entirely on a relationship for self-definition. The true love story, as we say, is the love among those women—and at many times, the men flitting in and out of their world were peripheral. It didn't matter if you adored Steve or hated

Aidan or had a not-so-secret appreciation for Trey. (I may be alone in that last camp, but I also love The Russian, so I'm used to being yelled at for my opinions.) What mattered is that you felt engrossed in these women's lives, stories, and personal happiness. When Samantha got diagnosed, you cried. When Charlotte put on that Elizabeth Taylor dress and made it to Brady's birthday, you yelled with joy. When Carrie had to drag her scraggly ass into Big's office to ask for money to save her apartment, a record scratched.

"Hold up, girl. This is a little degrading," you said, wondering why Carrie was consistently allowed to live a financial life not unlike a freshly caught fish, flailing and bouncing and gasping for oxygen on the wooden planks of an old trawler. Or maybe that was just me, but it really should be all of us. Because as the dust settles on the era of women's self-actualization, it's more important than ever that we start taking stock not just of the romantic and sexual questions posed by the show but also the financial ones. It's not enough that we just joke about how unaffordable their lives were, how unrealistic the portrait of NYC was, or how much each character would have had to spend each year on purses and shoes alone. We have to start digging into the individual characters' nuanced relationships to money and independence, because it isn't enough to just be the kind of woman who always has a condom in her Fendi. We know now that one must have goals and dreams that involve things like investments and property ownership and retirement, instead of just falling in love with your stumpy divorce lawyer.

And this is why, no matter how aspirational her wardrobe or enviable some of her flings (her character dated a young Bradley Cooper twice, as two different people!), Carrie is never the person we should be emulating. Nor is Charlotte, really, as her long-term financial strategy seemed to have been "date rich dudes, then date the rich dudes that help me divorce those previous rich dudes." It would be smarter to emulate Samantha, whose personal life may have been wild and unpredictable, but whose professional and financial security were always, for lack of a better word, tight. You couldn't shame Samantha because she had an iron grip over her own destiny and knew what she wanted—if that meant blowing the UPS guy in between closing seven-figure deals, that's exactly what she was going to do on a Tuesday.

But the person who feels, in my opinion, most aspirational for the TFD-er is Miranda. It's taken me a long time to come around to the fact that I am most definitely a Miranda, if only because the wardrobe department seemed to hate her so very much. But I am! I am a Miranda, and I love it, bucket hats and windbreakers and cowl-neck sweaters and all. I accept that I will be the one who runs out the door with mussed-up red hair and a swipe of burnt umber lipstick, ready to conquer the world. I'll be the one who loves her job, loves her friends (but isn't afraid to tell them when they're being huge dicks), and loves her life just the way it is. If that means I don't get some puffy white wedding dress or lavish ceremony to show how much I love my significant other, I'm okay with it. If I'm going to delay my fairy-tale ending to build some stability for myself, so be it. If I'm going to show up to brunch looking decidedly puffy sometimes because I spent the week eating Oreos, well, that's just how it's going to be. So, embrace your inner Miranda (but maybe not the eating-baked-goods-out-of-the-trash part).

TFD readers are savvy, practical, and goal-oriented, and they are constantly striving to get better on an individual level. They aren't afraid of brutal honesty when necessary, and are just as happy to swap info on their credit score as they are to talk about the hookup they had in a broom closet at the Portuguese Embassy the night before. So we're Mirandas, which is a wonderful thing to be. When it came to money and love, Miranda didn't take any shit. She would take her friends to task for their irresponsible financial choices, put a hard line between her money and her partner's until they committed, and, even then, she took the lead on big decisions because she was the one equipped to make them. Money, much like olive-colored, crew neck wool dresses, was no fucking joke to Miranda Hobbes. And it shouldn't be to us, either, especially when it comes to our relationships, romantic or otherwise. We should all strive to reach a level of openness, compassion, and serious personal boundaries when it comes to navigating money and love, and realize that talking about money doesn't make us assholes—*not* talking about money makes us idiots.

It's easy to have a vision of relationships floating along smoothly on some ethereal cloud of constant agreement and alignment, but the truth is, that almost never happens. Even if the two people in question are both mature, open, and respectful, what happens when one of them has way more money than the other? What happens when someone loses their job? What happens when somebody needs to borrow something, or someone doesn't pay the other person back? There are a million things that can go wrong with money between two people, and being squeamish about handling problems as they come up or keeping the money conversation open and fluid only hurts you in the end.

And when it comes to friendships, whether one-on-one or in a big social group, a disparity in income or relationship to money can be difficult to overcome. Often, in an effort to avoid any financial weirdness among friends, we avoid talking about money at all, assuming that the mention of hard numbers or goals or backgrounds might alienate someone—yet it's that very silence that stokes awkwardness and makes friends feel like they can't be honest with one another. Two friends with radically different incomes or spending habits aren't going to magically overcome that difference by ignoring it. The only way they can actually make it not that big of a deal is by confronting the issue head-on and talking about it as openly as they would anything else.

Socially and romantically, we know that conversation is the key to navigating differences and overcoming fears, but it can feel impossibly hard to be the one to start things off. What if we are the one who brings up salaries at brunch and suddenly seem like a vulgar, envious asshole? It shouldn't be risky to talk about these things, but it seems that even in our era of constant communication and over-sharing, money remains a taboo that even the most otherwise-open people refuse to really discuss. Over happy hour Prosecco, I asked my friend Anna Breslaw, author and former *Cosmopolitan* editor, what she thought about the whole "we'll talk about anything but money" phenomenon. As she put it, "I was a writer/editor at *Cosmo* for over two years, so I saw a lot of questions about deep, personal relationship shit. We had an attitude of 'no judgment, all topics are welcome,' and somehow, even with that attitude, we almost never heard questions about money unless we specifically sought them out. It sounds crazy, but people are more open to talking about anal sex than money."

It seems almost a ridiculous comparison to make, but the ease with which many of us discuss the physical aspects of relationships only serves to highlight the restrictions we have about money talk. We feel comfortable saying, "Women should demand orgasms,"

"It sounds crazy, but people are more open to talking about anal sex than money."

and yet we don't think (or say), "Women should demand their own, separate emergency fund in a relationship." We can think of a million boundaries and standards that we should have when it comes to the emotional and sexual parts of love, and yet be totally without those same standards for our finances.

I used to avoid the topic of money with friends, and especially with boyfriends, because I thought it vulgar at best and the stuff of excommunication at worst. And besides, I never brought anything to the relationship, financially, so when it came to long-term planning, I was pretty much at the whim of whomever I happened to be dating. It wasn't until I started talking about money regularly, and being more conscious of how I handled mine, that I realized I deserved that mutual level of respect and openness I sought to offer others. If I had a friend I could talk about literally everything with, yet never discuss numbers or goals because that was "taboo," how close were we, really? And if I was dating someone who wasn't willing to make financial planning a part of our life, where could our future actually go? Once I realized that talking about money is as much a part of a healthy relationship as talking about sex (or basically everything else people talk about when they care about each other), I got over the fear and dove right in over brunch with whatever friend I happened to be with. And this means that my close social circles have, over the past few years, become narrowed to the people with whom I can talk openly about money—but that's a good thing.

When you talk openly and honestly about money, you become more confident at work, more demanding of your own goals and habits, and more aware of what is and isn't healthy. Talking about money with friends helped me negotiate a good salary, and having a very financially open relationship with my partner allowed me to start my own business. Just like you'll have better sex by talking about it openly and asking questions, your financial life stands to be upgraded in the same way.

When I first started looking into the psychology behind talking about money in relationships, one name kept coming up over and over: Olivia Mellan. Olivia is the founder of Money Harmony, and a therapist and pioneer in the field of money conflict resolution. She's written or cowritten five books on the topic, and defined so much common knowledge on finance in relationships that she even has "laws" of money communication colloquially named after her. Her theories on navigating friendships and romantic relationships through the prism of financial health are simple, practical, and applicable to nearly everyone. And luckily for us, she was kind enough to sit down for a Q&A for this book. Here are her biggest and most important ideas on communication, independence, and when to call it a day.

Olivia MELLAN

Founder of Money Harmony, therapist and writer

Q. What are the biggest problems you see in relationships when it comes to money?

Generally speaking, the two biggest issues you tend to see are when a "Money Spender" is dating or married to a "Money Hoarder," and a "Money Worrier" is married to a "Money Avoider." And often, as you can imagine, those personality types tend to go hand in hand. And this polarization is extremely common— I've been talking couples polarization patterns around money and other areas for so long that people have started calling it "Mellan's Law," which is, "If opposites don't attract off the bat, which they usually do, then they will create each other eventually." This is a huge phenomenon in financial relationships—that these inherently different personality types drive one another, and become more pronounced over time. So even if two spenders get together, they'll fight each other for the super-spender, and the other will begin to save by comparison. And speaking generally, it's only in balancing these differences, and moving toward the middle, that you can have a happy partnership.

Q. Why do so many couples break up or divorce over money, in your opinion?

Over the past thirty years, money has been either the number one or number two cause of divorce in America. It's primarily because for most people, money is never just money. Money represents love, power, security, control, self-worth, self-esteem, freedom, and happiness. And so, as long as money is an emotionally loaded symbol, people can't make rational decisions about it. So that is why I teach my version of Harville Hendrix's "mirroring exercise." Step one: mirroring—playing back what the speaker said, as close to verbatim as possible; second step: validation—saying what makes sense about what your partner said, from his or her perspective; and step three: empathy ("I imagine you might also be feeling __ and __)—to truly enter your partner's world. You have to treat talking about money as compassionately and empathetically as you would talking about any emotional topic, because for most of us, money is emotionally loaded.

Q. Aside from constant and empathetic communication, what would you say is the most important strategy for navigating money in relationships?

All women need some separate money. All women need some separate money. All women need some separate money. And yes, I need to repeat it three times, because it's so crucial. And I say that because women's main challenge in relationships—I'm generalizing here, even financially—is over-giving and losing themselves in relationships. Most women learn to give themselves over entirely to their new identity and role as part of a couple. So I believe that keeping some separate money is a tangible, important symbol of some "self" that does not disappear in the relationship. On the other hand, many men who want to merge the money in a relationship reflect their biggest challenge—learning how to merge. Since often men have a hard time getting connected and staying connected, merging money is one way to lovingly express their desire for intimacy.

Q. And for friendships, what are the biggest money conflicts?

Really, there are two—very different financial status, and borrowing/lending money between friends. Now, that's not to say that this can't be overcome—it can. Two people from very different financial backgrounds can have a wonderful friendship, but they have to address that difference explicitly.

They have to acknowledge their difference and communicate it openly, because trying to pretend like it doesn't exist will only result in discomfort and conflicting needs. Empathetic communication is crucial in friendships as well as in primary relationships.

Q. But does that mean that lending money between friends is always a bad idea? As in, if you are two friends with seriously different incomes, should the friend with a lot more money never offer to help them out, financially?

My honest view is that you can, and sometimes you should, but the truth is that if you are lending money to someone in your life, you have to be comfortable with viewing that money as a gift. If you actually want to see that money back in full, and in a timely fashion, you shouldn't do it, because that's where relationships can get impaired or even destroyed.

Olivia's Steps for Working Out a Money Issue in Any Relationship

- Find a non-stressful time to have a money talk.
- Start with sharing an appreciation or two about each other— not necessarily about money.
- Each one should share something about how money was handled in their family of origin. The other should listen empathetically, without interruption.
- Share hopes and dreams—and fears and concerns. Play back what the other said, what makes sense about it from their perspective, what else they might be feeling.
- Only after feelings are shared, go to the "facts and figures."
- Agree not to attack each other or blame each other for problems related to money.
- End with an appreciation.

There are so many things that feel simply ugly when talking about money with people we love. Even if we weren't raised to feel like it's a taboo topic, it can often feel like if the relationship is good and right on its own merits, things like money issues will just sort of resolve themselves, because emotional connection should be strong enough to manage any "practical" problem. But as Olivia Mellan points out, money is almost never rational, and no relationship—no matter how wonderful it might be on a physical or emotional level—can magically overcome the logistical obstacles of life together. And this is true of romantic relationships, of course, but it's also true of friendships.

There are many friendships that begin, for example, when both parties are on a similar financial plane and then see a huge change of social standing over the course of even just a few years. They might have been a perfect match when they were both eating ramen and drinking vodka that comes in plastic bottles back in a college dorm, but what do those same friends do when one is dealing with massive debt and a low salary, and the other is making near six figures in their early twenties, with barely any debt to worry about? They're the same people, the reasons that they love each other as friends are likely the same, but it would be completely irrational to expect that these two people wouldn't have to seriously work at it to overcome the new money friction. Even if it's just a question of "I want to go on a vacation to Spain this summer" versus "I would like to manage to save at least a little bit of money this summer," the chances these friends have to run into unexpected issues are endless.

And that's why we have to remind ourselves regularly that it's not vulgar to talk about money with the people we love, even friends. In romantic partnerships, we're often forced to discuss money out of pure necessity, when we're moving in together or making big purchases or getting married. Partnerships mean almost inherently confronting money, even if you still find it an ugly topic. But friendships are much

easier to skate by on, convincing ourselves that the real crime would
be to identify the elephant in the room. It's up to us to confront that
idea, to talk about these issues, and to keep the conversation as open
as possible, because awkwardness between two people is only allowed
to grow and take root if no one acknowledges it. Speak your biggest
financial fears aloud, and they suddenly lose a lot of their power.

One of the people I most admire in my life is someone who has
had to confront tons of money ugliness out of necessity and has grown
to write openly about the topic over the past two years. Ashley Ford
is a prolific writer in New York City who grew up in near poverty in
Indiana and has risen to the upper echelons of the literary community,
putting her in tight circles with some of the most recognizable creative
names in the industry. Her rise in writing has been closely mirrored
by her socioeconomic rise, which would give many people money
whiplash. But Ashley has been determined to navigate it well, and that
has meant a lot of talking about money.

In part inspired by TFD and the conversation we've been
having over the past few years, Ashley has begun writing and living
with a constant openness about these financial differences and
acknowledging them head-on: yes, she grew up differently than a
lot of the New York creative world. No, that doesn't have to be a big
deal: Her partner grew up relatively privileged, some of her friends
are literal millionaires, and her own financial health has grown to
the point that she earns several times more than the highest amount
her mother ever earned. All of these realities are opportunities to feel
guilty, or awkward, or insecure, or shameful. Ashley has chosen none
of the above and has embraced a complete honesty about money that
has neutralized many of these potential land mines. She sat down with
me to talk about how she has approached money in relationships, and
no question was off-limits.

Ashley FORD

Writer

Q. Growing up poor and now moving around in relationships, friendships, and a socioeconomic bracket with wealthy backgrounds, do you ever feel awkward or frustrated?

Oh, I absolutely experience bewilderment at what people had available to them as kids and young people that I didn't; even people who get to study abroad in college. I couldn't fathom being able to study abroad in college because I'd always had two jobs the entire time I was in college. It's also things like the fact that I am dating someone who was able to travel internationally as a kid and a teenager. Sometimes he talks about it and I almost feel like my response is a little mean. I'd be like, "Oh, that time you saw all the pyramids and took a cruise down the Nile when you were seventeen." It hurts his feelings, and I have to temper myself, because he had the opportunity and appreciated it. And I am sort of letting the disparity in our experience create this chasm between us because I'm being flippant about it.

Q. Do you think that flippancy comes from feeling like the privilege a lot of people grew up with is treated almost like a moral or cultural achievement? Like people are somehow better for having more access?

Absolutely. The first article I ever wrote for a nationally printed magazine was about me going to England to learn about the Brontë sisters, but also the fact that this was my first trip outside the country, and that I never had the opportunity to do that before. So in talking about the excitement of my piece, I had a lot of people be like, "That is awesome, but what do you mean that was the first time you left the country? Weren't you like twenty-eight when that happened? The truth is I was twenty-nine. But the world I move around in now doesn't understand that so many people die without ever leaving the country. Most people do. My mother has never been on a plane, and she is not a rare case.

Q. Do you feel that a lot of you getting comfortable with talking about money over the past few years was having a partner with such a different socioeconomic background, and that kind of forced the conversation?
That was part of it. Another part of it was that I had mentors who made a lot more money than me. Like my big mentor is Roxane Gay, and you know Roxane Gay also made more money than me and has always been generous with me as far as making sure I had what I needed, to be perfectly honest. Or even being friends with people like Lena [Dunham] has meant that I have to get used to seeing money from such a radically different perspective, be okay with things like having someone pay for me and not feel guilty about it—it just doesn't make sense to not have certain people pay when we're out, but that can be a huge stumbling block if you grew up poor. But once you ac-knowledge that "Hey, we're just really different, financially, there's no reason that has to be weird," you can move on from it.

Q. When you look at the relationships you have, ranging from people back home who don't have the resources to fly somewhere, all the way up to people who are multimillionaires, what would you say has been the key to overcoming what could potentially be real stickiness?
I would say don't make it weird. When you talk about money with people in your life, don't treat it like a big, bad taboo thing. Make it very normal, and people will talk to you about it like it's very normal. At no point have I spoken with someone about money in a normal manner and had them rebuff me or not want to talk about it. So far, everyone has been very open—they seem, to be perfectly honest, kind of starved for it. People want to talk about money, but they just don't have anyone to talk about money with. People are scared to bring it up. But honestly, now, I can't imagine not talking about it.

Talking about money with the people we love can be absolutely terrifying, but it can ultimately be one of the most liberating things we do. We never want to end up like so many rom-com heroines before us, utterly bewildered by our own financial destinies, finding ourselves with hundreds of pairs of fabulous designer shoes but no 401(k), desperate for a man to come make sense of it all. And we also don't want to have our social circles slowly whittled down to "just the people who have the exact same salaries as I do," because that isn't how the world works. It's time we embraced a more pragmatic, thoughtful, and, yes, Miranda-like approach to money in relationships. We have to be unafraid of the implications, stop worrying about being perceived as "humorless," because we realize that not talking about money head-on is, in fact, no laughing matter. Ultimately, navigating our friendships financially/empathetically means keeping in mind one key reality: comfort.

We have to be acutely aware of where we stand on the spectrum of financial comfort. What do we consider "normal"? What do we consider "not a big deal"? What are our standards of living? What do we feel comfortable spending? What kind of safety net do we have and how does our financial future look? Are we drowning in debt? Building serious wealth? Earning well above six figures, or struggling on a first-year teacher's salary? Knowing how easy things are for you lets you know when the onus is on you to start the conversation, perhaps offer to pay for something, or divide something unequally. Accepting that not everyone has the same relationship to money out of necessity is hugely important to overcoming that divide, and being realistic about when you have privilege—and, yes, checking it—means always starting off on the right foot. Chances are, there is always someone we are more comfortable than, and if we all did our best to be aware of that and compensate for it, these conversations would happen much more organically.

When it comes to relationships, a key element to that same empathy is power. Who has the power in a relationship? Who has more income, has more wealth, is more financially educated and more comfortable being a decision maker? Who has a strong network of financial advice or security around them, and who doesn't? Who was raised to speak the language of money, and who wasn't? The unfortunate truth is that many women were not raised to have a lot of these tools, in addition to earning less at work, and may frequently find themselves in relationships where they are at a distinct financial disadvantage power-wise. Being with someone who acknowledges these differences, compensates for them, and looks to financial planning as a team activity and conversation rather than "I lead, you follow; you wouldn't understand" is essential.

Pop culture may have led us to believe that life should be a series of champagne brunches, Prince Charmings with black cards, and occasional money problems that magically sort themselves out in a neat two-episode arc, but real life is nothing like that. The point is, the only way we're going to have not just the relationships that satisfy us and evolve with us but the freedom to live that rich, fulfilling adult life is to be honest. We owe it to ourselves, and the people around us, to be open about our needs and our differences, and to not allow a little thing like money take a relationship down because we refuse to look it in the eye.

Money doesn't have to be a big deal unless we make it a big deal, but the only way we make it a big deal is by avoiding it and hoping it will go away. Money is sort of like the collective monster under our bed: the more we look away from it, the scarier it's going to get.

ACTION

Chapter 7

How to Build (and Pay for) Your Happiness

Give yourself permission to change your mind, and to start small.

When it comes to useless "inspirational" sayings, few are more blatantly dangerous than "Follow your dreams." Like a big red balloon, this phrase is bouncy and shiny and makes you happy just to think about it. But also like that balloon, it's generally empty, and liable to slip out of your hands, leaving you to watch it float away as you cry into your empty ice-cream cone (because your scoop of ice cream has also fallen on the ground in this metaphor). Empty inspirational sayings are one of the most dangerous things a young, ambitious woman can encounter because they don't just make you feel like you're failing to live up to your truest potential: they make you feel like you're an asshole for failing.

In the world of Pinterest, where quotes about travel are written over a picture of a Starbucks cup, good people get ahead. If you work hard, if you want something badly enough, if you chase your dreams relentlessly and with confidence, you succeed. In the absence of religion—and many of us have grown up without a lot of the structures and moral framework of organized religion—we have created this new kind of pseudo-spirituality that revolves vaguely around capitalism, and a narrow idea of creative expression. It's the spirituality that treats pretentious essays from CEOs about waking up at four a.m. to answer all their e-mails on a stationary bike as gospel instead of slightly insane. It's the spirituality that will forgive almost every life choice made in the pursuit of the capital-C Career—no matter how unbalanced or unsustainable—as inherently good, because it means that you're following your dreams.

As author Miya Tokumitsu of the brilliant book *Do What You Love* writes,

Passion as measured by hours has put the workweek on a course of runaway inflation, to the point at which people are actually

shortening their lives and endangering others—sometimes in sudden, tragic form—in pursuit of an ever-elusive ideal of capitalistic individualism.

Why do we allow ourselves to continue like this? If, according to the *Do What You Love* ethic, the pleasure of work derives from the very act of production, what are workers doing during all those surplus hours when they are not, well, producing, or producing only poorly? Why are salaried workers lingering in the office after their work is done or when they are beyond the point of meaningful production, only making themselves less effective in the long term?

The answer clearly has nothing to do with economic rationality and everything to do with ideology. Although simple Excel charts may present the flimsiest guise of empirical, objective data about workers' supposed passion, the truth is that passion doesn't equal hours spent in the office, nor does it necessitate burning oneself out. Passion is all too often a cover for overwork cloaked in the rhetoric of self-fulfillment.

Even if your capital-P Passion is not in the workplace, the single-minded pursuit of finding One Thing that will fulfill you and validate your life almost universally requires serious financial freedom. Nearly every dream that is vaunted in our society in this way—creative careers, entrepreneurship, extensive travel, elaborate hobbies—requires a good deal of financial freedom, if not at least security. In order to persue most Big Dreams, we need, if nothing else, a safety net to catch us if and when we fall. We need money.

We also need the time to dedicate to these pursuits, usually time that is unpaid in some way. Whatever it is that you're pursuing, you have to position yourself in a way that allows you to take a little risk, and calculating that risk is very different for different people. Can your parents help you financially? Can you live with them for a while? Do you have a spouse or partner who can support both of you? Do you have significant student debt or debt of any kind? Do you have a job you can drop to part-time and not be evicted from your apartment?

These are all very real questions, with very real answers that the dumb, faux-inspirational "follow your dreams" narrative completely flattens out of existence. We treat everyone the same, in this Pinterest version of libertarianism, where we all have the same abilities and obstacles, and our success or failure is entirely based on how hard we do or don't work. We pretend that "following your dreams" is the same call to action for the single mother with two part-time jobs and $40,000 in debt as it is for the trust-funder who wants to start an app while studying at Princeton. We act like traveling the world is something you can just do if you want to, as if it doesn't come with an enormous price tag that only the most privileged can afford. We pretend that the risks are the same for everyone, usually by not talking about the risks at all. Money is never a stumbling block in the "follow your dreams" narrative because its bullshit, house-of-cards philosophy would fall apart at the first mention of an actual number. Following your dreams costs a lot of money, and the reason why most successful entrepreneurs are white guys with wealthy parents isn't that they are somehow more passionate, or talented, or eager to work. It's that taking risks is about ten thousand times easier for those people. Period.

So what is the version of "follow your dreams" for people who are acutely aware that dream-following is an expensive, complicated endeavor? At TFD, we feel that "dreaming medium" was the perfect alternative to the frustratingly unattainable mantra of "dreaming big." We don't think that anyone should shy away from the things they want most in life, or that people should consider themselves excluded from the imagination game simply because they weren't born with a silver spoon. Everyone deserves to do what they love (to some extent), but the only way to remain sane and financially healthy while figuring out and executing what you love is to realize that it should entail *many* things—and doesn't need to happen all at once.

The reality is that many of us will have to do jobs we very much don't love, for some period of time, if not a very long time. For many of us, the idea of "doing what we love" is a very vague term. What does that even mean? We should do things that we love every day, sure, if we can, but the idea of that encompassing your career entirely seems dubious at best. So we propose that if we're going to dream medium, we have to give up that vague notion of getting *all* our fulfillment from one thing. We have to set our goals in little, manageable steps and embrace the idea that not all of our emotional eggs can be put in one basket. If we can love our jobs, relatively speaking, that's awesome. But we also need to love our friends and families and significant others and hobbies and time alone just reading or watching TV. We should diversify our fulfillment as much as possible, and not expect any one thing—even our Big Dreams—to make us suddenly feel whole.

So we believe in dreaming medium not just because it makes it easier for one to pursue one's goals but because it breaks down that chase into steps—and creates enough mini-goals within the journey—so that you don't have time to become overly preoccupied by one single thing. Dreaming medium also allows you to chase more than one goal at a time and to spread out your definition of success into many individual components, to diversify your sources of fulfillment and happiness, and measure your wealth much more in freedom than in dollars.

Something else we've figured out at TFD is that a big part of taking the first step on the path toward a dream is realizing that others have gone there before—and that there is nothing inherently special or unique about those people. One woman who embodies this view is my friend Akilah Hughes, who has managed to diversify and reassess her creative and professional paths more than anyone I know. By any standards, she's achieved considerable success with her filmmaking and writing careers, and could easily rest on her laurels by now and cruise toward a corner office— yet each time I see her, she is doing something different and testing out her own abilities. And unlike many of the people around her, she grew up decidedly unprivileged, financially, and had no easy in for the work she wanted to do. There was no one to hook her up with an internship (even unpaid) or informational interview.

As she put it, "I was the kind of person who did a lot of research on the people who I looked up to, in terms of performing, and it became obvious immediately that so many people have a dad that was like a filmmaker, or they grew up in LA, so they were consistently in front of people. There were so many benefits you could have just from the access you had. And I had to give up the idea that we were both starting from zero and had the same obstacles—we don't. I can't have the straight line they do, but I can still do it.

"At some point, you have to accept that you can be the person who does the thing you want to do, and that there are so many people already doing what you want to do who are objectively not that great. It's a self-preservation thing—you have to say to yourself, and accept that it's not a bad thing to say: 'I know that I am good enough for this, because I'm better than many people who are already there. I just haven't been in the right place in front of the right people yet.'"

The mantra of "I deserve to try" is perhaps the biggest weapon we have against the inherent unfairness of the universe. Figuring out how you can compensate for wherever you may be positioned on the staggered starting line of life, and then feeling deserving of being part of the race, are things we all have to get used to. From day one of Akilah's young adult life, pursuing the things she loved was tempered by working enough to support it. "It didn't even occur to me as unusual," she said. "I've just always known that you have to work your way toward things."

We all have to work. If you're reading this, chances are you are not some trust-funder in neon Ray-Bans whose only concern is which angle they look best in when posing for selfies on their yacht. We have to work, and attacking the dreams we have is going to take a lot of planning. Though taking exciting financial risks can be fun, the fun generally stops when you're googling "Selling organs legal [insert your state here]?" to pay your rent.

Unless you are very, very lucky, getting what you want isn't going to be some fairy-tale narrative—the stories are messy and the results are never exactly what we expect them to be, but the thread that connects them all is the same: prepare for the unexpected, be ready to work harder, and don't put all your happiness in one basket. There isn't a perfect, catchall guidebook to achieving your goals, but there are some basic rules we should all play by.

From running TFD, and talking to our many experts, I've come up with what I believe is the most reasonable, doable "follow your dreams" playbook for people who can't afford to be stupid. It's your Starter Kit for Happiness, some assembly required.

Starter Kit for Happiness

#1.
Decide what you want your life to look like on a day-to-day basis: What hours do you want to work? What hobbies do you want to have? What career path interests you? What are your financial goals? Relationship goals?

#2.
Whatever your loftiest goals and dreams are, break them into several mini-dreams and tackle them one by one (celebrating each victory as it comes).

#3.
Identify the places where you want to take risks or make changes, and will need a safety net.

#4.
Create a detailed, thoughtful budget and yearly financial plan that takes into account both day-to-day costs and your longer-term financial goals.

#5.

When it comes to risks and changes, start planning specifically for them at least a year in advance: anything from a move to a new city to a completely new career path needs to be thought through and well planned, financially and logistically.

#7.

Give yourself freedom to change your mind—if you decide that world travel or oil painting isn't all you thought it would be, accept that it doesn't define who you are. If a great and unexpected opportunity comes along, you are allowed to take it. Adjust your plans as life dictates.

#6.

Once you have your year long plan, break it down into month-to-month steps full of actionable items and goals.

#8.

Stick to your budget through as much volatility as you can— if your lifestyle is preventing you from saving money, it had better be very temporary.

#9.

Remember that you are good enough to try for the things you want, and do not let a less-advantaged background or inexperience dissuade you from at least attempting something.

#10.

A casual hobby could become an awesome career (points to self with both thumbs).

#11.

Accept your class privileges or obstacles where you have them.

#12.

Diversify your income and skill set by always maintaining at least one side gig—look at your path through the profes-sional world as a lattice, and not a ladder.

#13.

Learn to do things for yourself, and let your home life become both a key part of your fulfillment and a key part of saving some serious money: everything from making your own food to building your own furniture can and should be on your list of "cool, affordable shit I enjoy doing."

#14.

Be honest and thoughtful about money in all your relationships—share your dreams and help each other figure out how to get there, in practical ways.

#16.

Live below your means, and remember to be impressed by shit. Your life is probably pretty fucking awesome, but even the coolest life would seem dull if your expectations and spending habits way exceeded it.

#15.

Accept that you may not get what you want every time and that the thing you thought would make you happy might leave you feeling completely "meh." Learn to have a diverse-enough portfolio of fulfillment and joy that no one disappointment, professional or otherwise, is enough to make you feel seriously thrown off your path.

#17.

Be kind, most of all, to yourself.

Follow the Rule of Four:
Always have at least four concrete, tangible things you can point to in your life that are as defining, fulfilling, and important as your work—diversify your sources of happiness.

These rules are not a guarantee of the life you want, but they are the building blocks to help you get there. As I've said before, money doesn't buy you happiness, but it buys you the Lego kit of happiness. It buys you comfort, security, and options, even if you still have to build your happiness on top of it. And these rules are simply an extension of that—if nothing else, they provide you with the closest thing possible to a blank life canvas.

Over the past few years, I've learned that to be good with money is like a good long-term relationship. Instead of everything being chaotic peaks of highs and lows, there is a more quiet, sustained happiness that allows you to plan for the future, feel safe and comfortable, and really figure out what you want in life. I have learned to approach money in the way I approach my most treasured relationships— forgiving human mistakes, setting small goals, celebrating the milestones along the way. I have given up this idea of "dreaming" when it comes to money, imagining that some future version of myself will magically have it all together, and that I'll both end up rich somehow and know exactly what to do with that wealth. I know that Future Me is someone I have to build every day, someone I have to pay and plan for and adjust as I go. I dream medium with my money because I know what goals are realistic for me and what behaviors are realistic for a flawed human like myself. I also know that financial success will only be one part of a much bigger picture, and I don't expect it to solve my problems or make me into a better person.

One of the people who inspires me most in this way, who really embraces this idea of balancing your life, treating money as a means to do more of what you love, and not getting all your fulfillment in one place, is Hank Green. Aside from being one of the first ever fans (and partners!) of TFD, Hank is one of the most traditionally "successful" people on the Internet—he does everything from make videos for tens of millions of subscribers to organize and headline mind-bogglingly big creative conventions—yet when I met him in person for the first time in New York, he'd just come from Uniqlo, where he was very excited about buying himself a new jacket for the winter. He is someone who could afford to shop in any luxury store on Fifth Avenue and yet was happy to have just what he needed, and do other, more fulfilling things with that money.

And, more important, Hank is someone whose path to such (frankly) staggering success is not some perfect, straight line. I admit (with some level of embarrassment) that when I was first made aware of him, I assumed he must have come from serious money. I assumed that anyone who had reached the levels of creative success he had must have had some angel investor somewhere, some loaded family member who decided, "Hey, this thing my kid is doing is awesome, I'm going to throw money at it." And while that is true for many media entrepreneurs, and it would be naive to think otherwise, learning about Hank's path taught me that my assumptions were unfair, and that learning a person's actual story is always worth the effort, and much better than blindly assuming.

Hank's initial approach to pursuing his own dreams is something that most of us could learn from, and he was kind enough to share some of his own approach to navigating limited funds, chasing big ideas, and finding happiness in it all. Here's what Hank has to say:

Hank GREEN

Video maker. Cocreator of Complexly, DFTBA, and VidCon

It might feel like I've been an Internet person all my life, but I didn't initially quit my job to become a blogger—I quit my job so that I could move to Montana with my girlfriend. I came out here and my goal was to get a job, which I was pretty unsuccessful at. So, through maybe five to six small sources of income after the first few months, I was sustainable. But it's pretty cheap to live out here. Rent is like five hundred dollars a month, and I lived very simply, and I always kept a small amount of fallback money—so when the traditional jobs weren't working out, and I didn't have one "serious" thing, I could pursue my blog. Initially, it was making maybe twenty dollars a month, but I had started it in grad school and was more interested in the experience of making it than the money it could bring—it started as a class project. But within a few years, especially around the time *An Inconvenient Truth* came out and there was buzz around environmental sites like mine, I was able to focus solely on the blog. Between that and a few other creative freelance jobs, I made seventeen thousand dollars in 2007. That was an amount that was sustaining me, and it's grown from there—but if I hadn't been okay with living on a small amount of money, I almost certainly wouldn't have been able to do it. So I kept manageable finances, but I also focused on the things that were actually interesting me, not some specific path or person I wanted to imitate. I think that is often a huge pitfall, like "I want to be like Tina Fey, and I'm going to work hard to follow in her footsteps." That's super problematic for structuring your career, because every career is different, and the world changes very fast right now. You should take the tools that other people have, and the lessons they've learned, but you shouldn't take the path, because it will never be exactly the same for you. The things that worked for them may not work for you. So personally I've found that, if I'm not learning from something or finding some element of success to it, I just abandon it— even if it's something I felt so sure that I wanted. I just move on. You can't be married to any one idea or path—my in-box is littered with abandoned ideas. You should see the number of domain names I have registered just because they were puns.

I think that being realistic about your goals, and what they will give you, is part of growing up, to some extent. You realize that the "magical" things aren't magical and that everything is made up of people, and people are made up of a combination of experiences and ideas and some of those things are good, and some are bad, and it's just complicated. I think that you find your passions in other, different things as you get older, and those things might feel more mundane to you right now. But you realize, in a way, that it's harder for young people, because just because something doesn't seem unique to you, it often seems sort of bland. It's easy to forget that those more "mundane" dreams that everyone has can still be extraordinarily valuable and worth fighting for.

We often talk as a society about how hard young people work to make their dreams come true, that we work like eighty hours a week to pursue that professional fulfillment. But I don't think anyone works harder than a new mom, and her passion is no less a passion—we just don't talk about it in those terms. But it's the same drive, it's just a different expression, it's more subdued. I recognize that there are times when things will happen to me now that five years ago or ten years ago would have been like "I cannot believe the thing that just happened to me! I need to run up and down my house and shout to the whole neighborhood this cool thing!" and now I'm like "I don't know if I want to do that." And that's fine.

Accepting that has been a process for me: realizing that not everything has to be these enormous highs and lows has been a long process. And ultimately I think that accepting that is basically like being married. I am never going to fall in love again like I did when my wife and I first fell in love. We are never going to feel that same combination of feelings, but we feel different feelings that are stronger and safer and full and rich and wonderful. I would not trade that for anything.

"I've found that, if I'm not learning from something or finding some element of success to it, I just abandon it—even if it's something I felt so sure that I wanted. I just move on. You can't be married to any one idea or path—my in-box is littered with abandoned ideas. You should see the number of domain names I have registered just because they were puns."

I challenge you to ask yourself, as honestly as you can, what you really want out of your life—not just the "big" things, but how you want your average day to look and what you want to be doing with it. Ask yourself what places you want to go, what meals you want to cook, where you want to be living and who you want to be living with. Figure out what you need to feel safe and comfortable, to be truly independent in the best sense of the word. Answer all these things to yourself honestly, and figure out how you can use money as a tool to get you there. Commit to viewing money not as something to hoard but something to cushion yourself with and propel yourself forward. Know that you will have a million different passions and desires and dreams in life and that being savvy with money will be the difference between never giving yourself permission to pursue them and being able to live them out.

Dream medium, keep a checklist, and remember to drink lots of water. That's the Financial Diet we all should be on.

Glossary

Bond:

A form of debt; borrowed money that needs to be repaid, most often with interest. Debt securities come with the promise that lenders would be paid back first, resulting in debt securities tending to be less risky and more stable than equity. In exchange for that preferential treatment, lenders receive what is typically a lower but more consistent return.

Broker (in the context of a home):

A broker is someone who acts as a middleman between a seller and a buyer of real estate/real property. Their job is to find sellers who are interested in selling property and finding buyers who are interested in buying.

Broker (in the context of finance):

In finance, a broker is someone who buys and sells securities on a stock exchange on behalf of clients.

Credit score:

A numerical score—ranging from 300 to 850 that represents your creditworthiness, how trustworthy you are with money.

Day trading:

The act of buying and selling financial instruments within the same day.

Deductible:

A tax deductible is a reduction in tax obligation from a taxpayer's gross income.

Diversification:

A risk management strategy that seeks to decrease the volatility of a portfolio by including a number of investments in different areas. Diversification reduces the risk that poor performance of a single company or industry, or a downturn in any one region, will significantly lower the value of your portfolio, for example, investing in a tech company, a bank, and a utility.

Down Payment (for mortgage):

In terms of a mortgage, it's the first payment you make on the loan. Most mortgage lenders require a down payment of at least 3 percent and can go up to about 20 percent.

Emergency Fund:

A specific stash of money that you set aside to pay bills in case of an emergency— like a medical emergency or a job loss.

Exchange Traded Fund (ETF):

An investment fund that tracks a stock or bond index or the value of a commodity. Unlike actively managed funds, ETFs typically have low expenses due to their passive investment strategy and low turnover of securities in the fund.

FHA Loan:

A mortgage insured by the Federal Housing Administration that includes mortgage insurance, paid by the borrower, that protects the lender in case of failure to pay. These loans generally allow for a lower down payment to secure the mortgage.

Fiscal:

Relating to government revenue, or taxes.

Financial Adviser:

Someone who provides financial advice and/or guidance for clients. They typically have a license for practicing as a professional financial adviser.

Guarantor:

In the context of leasing property, a lease guarantor is a third party involved to provide additional security within a rental agreement. The lease guarantor is someone who signs their name to the contract and agrees to pay if the tenant is not able to pay the rent.

Hard credit inquiry:

A hard inquiry is when your credit history is pulled for review because you've applied for some kind of credit—too many of these negatively impact your credit score.

Hedge fund:

A company that invests pooled funds of qualified individuals, and that uses various higher-risk strategies to generate active returns for said investors.

Index Fund:

A type of mutual fund with a portfolio constructed to match or track the components of a market index.

Investment:

Something that's purchased with the hope that it will generate income or will appreciate in the future.

Investment Return:

The profits from an investment, including all income and capital gains.

Liquidity:

The degree to which an investor may quickly buy or sell an asset without having a material impact on its price. Liquid markets are characterized by a high volume of activity.

Mortgage:

Simply put, it's a loan used to buy a home. The loan provides people with the money to buy the house, and the loan is guaranteed by the house. A loan provided by a bank or other creditor in exchange for the title to the debtor's property, where the title returns to the debtor upon full repayment of the loan.

Mutual Fund:

A type of investment fund that is managed by a professional money manager who invests the fund's capital in a diversified portfolio according to the objectives and strategies outlined by the fund. Mutual funds allow investors to invest in diversified portfolios that could be difficult to construct with a small amount of capital, and to also benefit from professional management.

Property Tax:

A property tax is a tax assessed on real estate, and something that's determined by the value of the property and set by the local/municipal government.

Renter's Insurance:

An insurance policy that serves to protect some of the assets and activities of the renter of a given property.

Rule of 72:

A simple rule to determine how long an investment will take to double. Simply divide the number 72 by your compound annual interest rate. (And remember, a rate of 5 percent would be expressed as 5, not .05.)

Savings:

Savings is simply money that has been set aside for a future use, determined or otherwise.

Side hustle:

Paying work you take on outside of your regular job to increase your revenue and/or strengthen your skill set.

Stocks:

Stocks represent ownership interests in a company and the equity value available to shareholders after all debts are settled. Stocks provide investors with the opportunity for their ownership stakes to become more valuable as their companies generate more profits, but equity is also riskier than debt, exposing investors to the risk that their investments will decrease in value if the company performs below expectations or, worse yet, a bankruptcy wipes out their shares.

Volatility:

Measures how much the value of a stock or other security has fluctuated over time. Securities with higher volatility are riskier, but also typically offer the potential for bigger gains (or bigger losses). More stable ones are less likely to provide much more than a modest return.

Property taxes:

A tax levied on the value of a property, usually real estate.

Aknowledgments

Chelsea and Lauren would like to thank:

Jim, Fuller, Mark, and Karen for being incredibly supportive and encouraging parents throughout the book-making process. To Libby for being a warm, thoughtful, and dizzyingly talented editor, to Anthony for being the perfect example of what a true advocate and friend in this industry should be, and to the whole team at Henry Holt for believing in this book as much as we did. Thank you, last, to the TFD team — Holly for being the endlessly positive backbone of our site, Annie for always seeing things bigger and better than we can, and Mary for reminding us to stay hungry and curious.

We love you all.

Index

Chelsea Fagan

Chelsea is a writer and cofounder of *The Financial Diet*. After not graduating from college, she began her writing career at Thought Catalog, where she spent three years before starting *The Financial Diet* as a personal side blog in August 2014. In between, she's written for dozens of outlets, including *The Atlantic, Cosmopolitan, VICE*, and *Grantland*, and published a first book, *I'm Only Here for the WiFi*. She lives in New York City with her fiancé and her dog, Mona, where she spends most of her free time cooking and convincing people to go dancing with her.

Lauren Ver Hage

Lauren is an art director and cofounder of *The Financial Diet* living and working in NYC. She graduated from Ramapo College of New Jersey with a major in Visual Communication Design, and from there worked as an art director at an advertising agency and as a freelance designer for Nickelodeon, before moving on to cofound *The Financial Diet*. This is her first foray into book design, which she could not be more thrilled about. She enjoys typography, sketching, baking, and making cocktails with her husband in their (very) cozy apartment. She also desperately wants a dog. (Stay tuned.)